Sacred Grove Press

© Melanie Fitz-Gerald, Bryony Simmonds

All rights reserved. No part of this publication may be reproduced or transmitted in any form or by any means electronic, mechanical, photocopying, recording or otherwise, without the prior written permission from the publisher. The views expressed in this book are not necessarily the views of the publisher.

Original text by Melanie Fitz-Gerald
Edited by Bryony Simmonds and Jane Church

First published in 2024

ISBN 978-1-915495-48-8 (paperback)
ISBN 978-1-915495-41-9 (e-book)

Published by
Sacred Grove Press Limited
NE48 3LT, Wark, Northumberland, UK
www.sacredgrovepress.co.uk

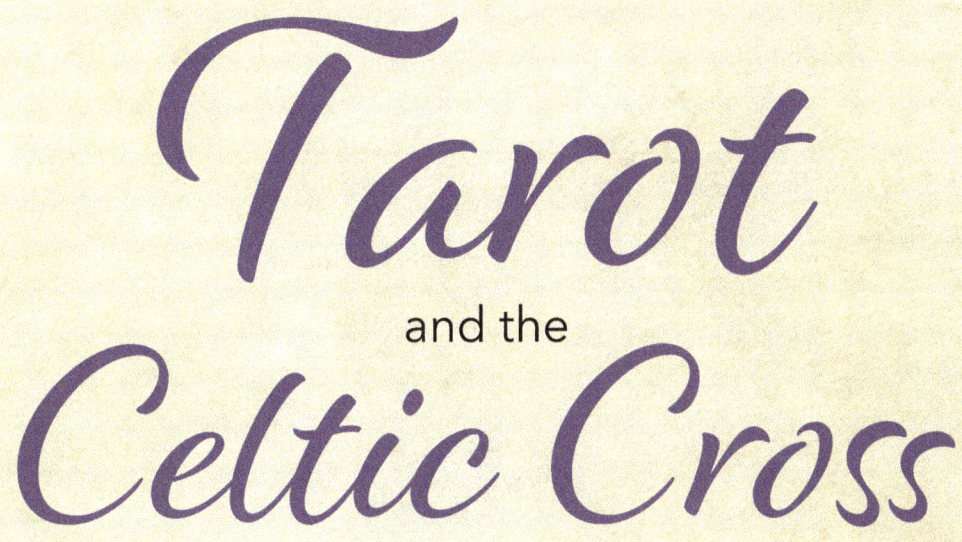

Meanings for every card in every position

Original text by Melanie Fitz-Gerald
Edited by Bryony Simmonds and Jane Church

Sacred Grove Press

This book has been published in loving memory of

Melanie Fitz-Gerald

Born Melanie Ursula Van Den Berg, Mel was a very considerate and caring person, with a love of animals. She was really like a big sister to me, and I miss her. She married Gerald Fitz-Gerald, a musician of note. Her marriage was a match made in heaven and they were married until he died. She still spoke to him after his death, missed him right up until she also passed.

Wonderful mother and wife. Rest in peace.

Shaun Fitz-Gerald

About the Author

Melanie Fitz-Gerald was a passionate scholar of mystical arts, whose lifelong exploration of Tarot and numerology culminated in a profound and accessible guide to the Celtic Cross spread. Born in Johannesburg, South Africa, in 1945, Melanie's journey was as rich and intricate as the divination practices she mastered.

She travelled with her musician husband Gerald, who performed at Southern Sun hotels throughout South Africa during the vibrant cultural landscape of the seventies and eighties. In her free time, she delved deep into the mysteries of spiritual practice, developing an extraordinary understanding of Tarot that would become her lasting legacy.

Her fascination with numerology, mysticism, and ancient civilisations—particularly Egypt and Israel—shaped her unique approach to divination. After decades of study and teaching, Melanie developed a comprehensive method of Tarot reading that demystifies this complex spiritual tool, making it accessible to practitioners of all levels.

Melanie passed away in her beloved home in Durban, KwaZulu Natal, leaving behind a rich legacy that continues to inspire and guide those drawn to the transformative power of Tarot.

Foreword

This book is based on a tarot course designed by my grandmother, Melanie Fitz-Gerald.

Through decades of study and teaching, Mel devised meanings for every Major Arcana card in every position of the Celtic Cross. I worked with her notes for many years and found they enhanced my understanding of the Tarot and make readings easier.

Realising the value of having a specific placement meaning, I expanded Mel's original text to include meanings for all the Minor Arcana cards as well.

These meanings are not meant to be limiting, but rather to give you a starting point to understand a card in any position. To get a complete answer, it will also be useful to read the rest of the card's information and consider the surrounding cards, reinforcing cards and opposing cards.

Each card has a double-page spread, which includes:
- keywords
- a description of the card and symbols used
- definitions for all the various types of readings (love, career, and spiritual)
- 12 unique meanings for every Celtic Cross position
- reinforcing and opposing cards

I truly believe that this book will elevate your Tarot reading experience and make you confident and proficient in no time.

When working with divination tools, remember that they offer guidelines not instructions and you should always use your common sense.

The meanings in this book focus on the Celtic Cross spread. This is probably the oldest and most popular Tarot spread, which offers a simple but powerful reading. You can also adapt the meanings to use for other spreads.

Bryony Simmonds

Welcome to the Tarot

The world of the Tarot is a fascinating one, and I hope you enjoy every minute of your adventure in it.

A deck of Tarot cards consists of 78 cards. These are divided into 2 parts – the Major Arcana and the Minor Arcana. The Major Arcana consists of 22 cards which represent major life lessons. The Minor Arcana is divided into 4 suits (Cups, Pentacles, Swords and Wands), each containing 14 cards.

Tarot can be used for a variety of purposes. It is most commonly used to give glimpses of the future, but also for understanding the hidden influences of a situation and receiving advice on the best way forward.

TAROT DECKS
I have used the popular Rider-Waite Tarot cards in this book. However, there are numerous Tarot decks available and you can use any with this book.

STORING AND CARING FOR YOUR CARDS
How you care for your cards is a personal preference. Mine are wrapped in black silk, other people keep them in their original box. Some cleanse them before every use, some people sleep with their cards under their pillow for the first week. Mel always insisted on sorting her cards back into order after each use. Do what feels right for you.

DOING A READING
When you are ready, hold the cards and close your eyes. Concentrate on your question, and say it aloud if that feels appropriate. Keep your question in mind as you shuffle the cards.

When you feel that the cards are sufficiently shuffled, place the deck face down before you. Cut the deck by moving some cards to create a pile to the left. Cut the deck again, moving a pile of cards to the right. Sometimes, the deck will only allow itself to be split twice, which is fine; let the cards dictate.

Regroup the cards in a quick motion without giving it too much thought. Holding the full deck, begin to place cards from the top of the deck according to your chosen spread. Turn over the cards as you place them.

When all the cards are laid out, look at the spread as a whole. Do any suits dominate? Are there any court cards or Major Arcana cards? Are any numbers predominant? Write down your initial feelings. Then turn to each card's page in the book, and read the meanings, noting any opposing or reinforcing cards.

CARD INTERACTIONS
In a reading, the cards interact with each other. The presence of one can alter or reinforce the meaning of another. I've included opposing and reinforcing card meanings for each.

REVERSED CARDS
Neither Mel nor myself believed in different meanings for reversed cards. Originally, the Tarot was not meant to be read reversed as most situations are already represented by the 78 cards in a deck.

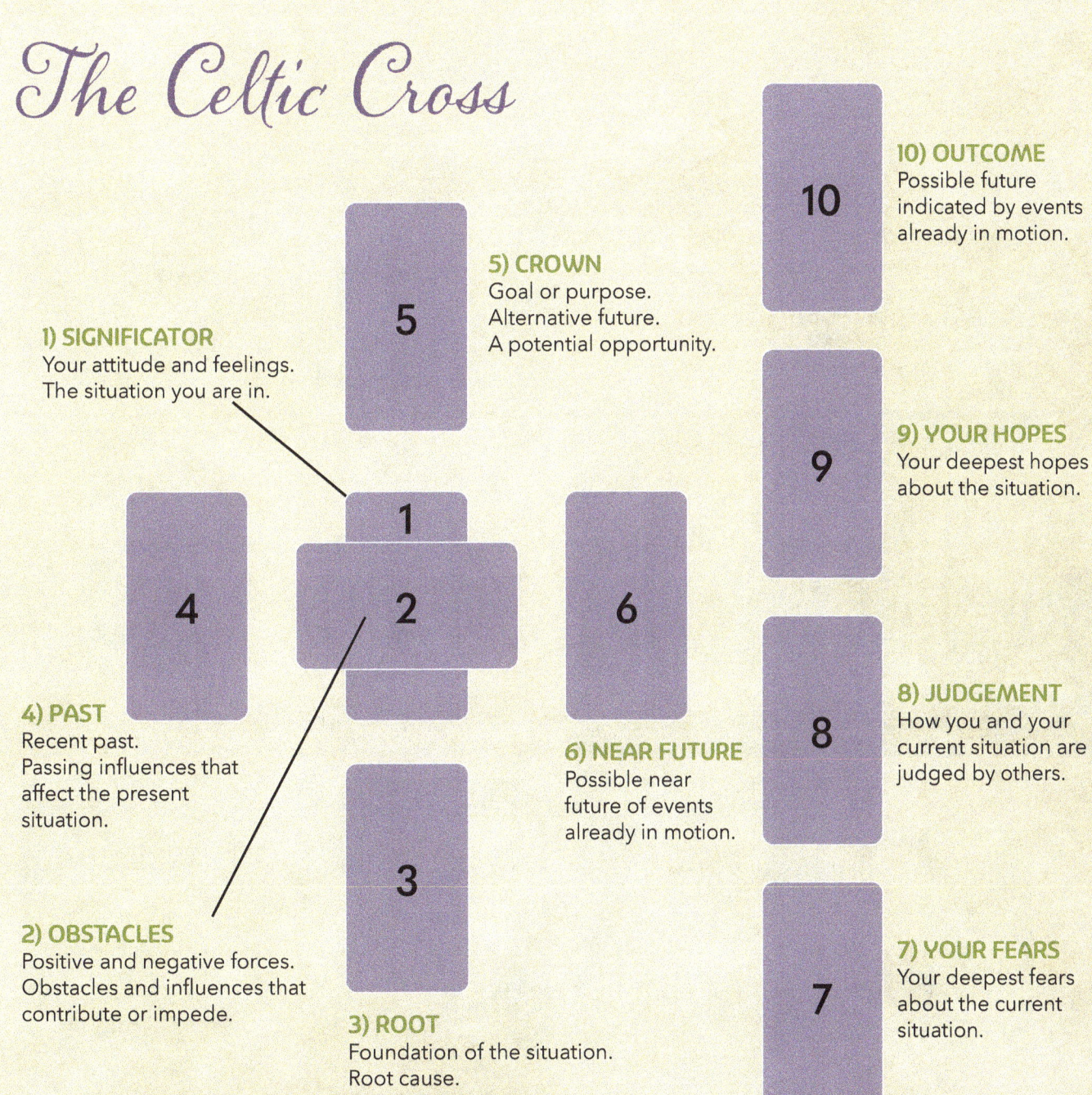

The Major Arcana

The Major Arcana consists of 22 cards which represent essential life lessons and experiences. Each of these has a name and a number. Major Arcana cards in your reading imply that the current issue is important.

0 THE FOOL
beginnings, naïvety, spontaneity, blind faith

1 THE MAGICIAN

action, communication, concentration, skill

2 THE HIGH PRIESTESS

inaction, inner wisdom, deeper mysteries

3 THE EMPRESS

motherhood, creativity, abundance, nature

4 THE EMPEROR

fatherhood, structure, authority, leadership

5 THE HIEROPHANT

tradition, belief systems, conformity

6 THE LOVERS

relationships, sexuality, personal beliefs, choices

7 THE CHARIOT

conquest, hard control, willpower, self-assertion

8 STRENGTH

inner strength, soft control, patience, determination

9 THE HERMIT

introspection, solitude, contemplation, guidance

10 WHEEL OF FORTUNE

destiny, opportunities, movement, new cycle

11 JUSTICE

fairness, decisions, cause and effect, justice

12 THE HANGED MAN

letting go, patience, surrender, sacrifice

13 DEATH
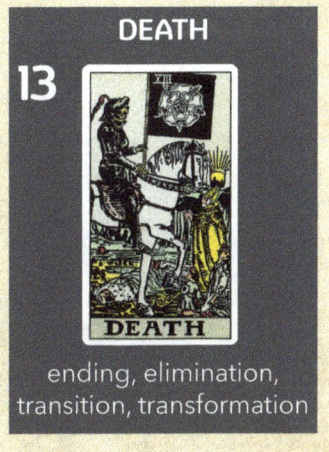
ending, elimination, transition, transformation

14 TEMPERANCE

balance, moderation, compromise, combining

15 THE DEVIL

temptation, materialism, oppression, hostility

16 THE TOWER

change, catastrophe, chaos, enlightenment

17 THE STAR

hope, inspiration, optimism, renewal

18 THE MOON

dreams, imagination, fear, bewilderment

19 THE SUN

enlightenment, growth, abundance, happiness

20 JUDGEMENT

judgement, rebirth, inner calling, karma

21 THE WORLD

completion, fulfilment, spiritual attainment

• BEGINNINGS • FREEDOM • NAÏVETY • FAITH • SPONTANEITY • IMPULSIVENESS • OPTIMISM

0 The Fool

At its heart, The Fool symbolises taking a leap of faith and having blind trust. He is at the beginning of a new cycle and does not yet have experience, so he goes as a fool – trusting and naïve. The Fool looks around with wonder and sees possibilities everywhere. He is also unpredictable and tends to rush into things.

OVERVIEW
The Fool encourages us to be optimistic, to take a leap of faith and to explore outside our comfort zone. With The Fool, anything is possible. This card represents a fresh start and an unexpected adventure.

LOVE
If you are in a relationship, The Fool is not necessarily a good omen, as he is unpredictable and spontaneous. If you are single, The Fool may hint at a whirlwind, impulsive and carefree romance. We often become The Fool when we fall in love – we can be overcome by emotion and are blind to potential conflict or incompatibilities. It can also suggest being inconsiderate towards other people.

CAREER
In a career reading, The Fool suggests movement. A change is coming – perhaps a new job or career is on your horizon, or a new project has grabbed your attention. The Fool is full of creative energy and new ideas. However, this card warns of the dangers of rushing into things without thinking them through.

SPIRITUALITY
The Fool can indicate the beginning of a spiritual journey. He encourages you to trust your intuition and take a leap of faith.

ADVICE
Being unpredictable and carefree can negatively affect those around you. Make sure that your attitude isn't causing unnecessary harm.

DESCRIPTION
A man has embarked upon a journey. His eyes are closed, his face tilted towards the sky. He doesn't seem to realise how close he is to the edge of the cliff. He holds a white rose, representing his purity and innocence. He carries what little he needs in his satchel. The small white dog, symbolising loyalty and protection, either encourages him to take the next step or tries to warn him. In the background, the mountains represent challenges yet to come.

• INNOCENCE • ADVENTURE • PLAYFULNESS • FOOLISHNESS • PURITY • CHILD-LIKE • TRUSTING

Celtic Cross Positions

1. **SIGNIFICATOR:** You are willing to take risks. Eager, innocent, optimistic and open-minded. You are searching for something meaningful in life.

2. **OBSTACLES:** Represents poorly planned or thought-out actions. Spontaneity, irrationality or naïvety. Being a fool without a plan, purpose or goal.

3. **ROOT:** The current situation has been caused by a foolish decision or an unruly sense of adventure.

4. **PAST:** You acted like a fool or made decisions that now seem foolish.

5. **CROWN:** You are open to new situations and trust others. A warning that it can be dangerous to act before thinking things through.

6. **NEAR FUTURE:** Follow your heart, dreams and intuition. You may be embarking on an adventure or a new way of life and abandoning the old. It suggests that you may have come to a crossroads and need to decide which direction you want to go in.

7. **FEAR:** You fear letting go, of being out of control. A fear of acting without knowing all the facts. A fear of the unknown. A fear of being taken for a fool.

8. **JUDGEMENT:** In a negative light, others see you as a foolhardy person who acts before thinking or jumps from one thing to another. In a positive light, you are considered open, innocent and trustworthy.

9. **HOPE:** Represents a desire to be free, to come and go without restrictions or responsibilities.

10. **OUTCOME:** It suggests moving on and choosing your own path. An adventure or an opportunity. Following your intuition and your heart. A big decision and change of direction lie ahead. An exciting time. Be ready for anything.

OPPOSING CARDS

JUSTICE
routine,
following convention

DEATH
ending,
closing down

THE DEVIL
feeling cynical,
lack of faith

TWO OF SWORDS
holding back,
blocking off experience

FOUR OF PENTACLES
order,
regularity

REINFORCING CARDS

THE HANGED MAN
having faith,
going with the flow

THE STAR
innocence,
faith, trust

JUDGEMENT
rebirth,
new beginnings

THREE OF WANDS
expanding horizons,
unexplored territory

• COMMUNICATION • ACTION • POWER • PERSUASION • CONCENTRATION • SKILL • DIRECTION

1 The Magician

The Magician is the symbol of creation. He is a practical achiever with a clear purpose, and turns ideas into reality. The Magician represents learning, skills and action. He suggests that now might be the time to act and follow your dreams.

OVERVIEW
When The Magician appears, it is time for action. You have the skills, willpower and resources you need. The choices you make now can lead to significant changes in your life. If you can let go of self-doubt and worry, success could be yours.

LOVE
The Magician bodes well if you are in a relationship but reminds you that constant effort is required. If you are single, The Magician hints at new prospects on the horizon.

CAREER
The Magician brings positive energy to your work life. New ideas and plans are likely to be surging through you. The Magician encourages you to put your ideas into action. It might be a good time to start a business or launch a new project.

SPIRITUALITY
It is a good time for spiritual development when The Magician appears. This card suggests that intuition and inspiration are currently flowing through you.

ADVICE
You might get so swept up in the next project or idea that you neglect yourself and those close to you. Make sure you find a balance between your work and personal life.

DESCRIPTION
The Magician points his wand to the sky with his right hand. The index finger of his left hand points to the Earth. This symbolises the merging of energies above and below. Above him, the sideways figure eight (representing balancing opposing forces). His belt is a serpent devouring its tail, (eternity). In front of him, the Minor Arcana are shown by the range of experiences described by these four suits. In the foreground are red roses (desire) and white lilies (purity).

• CREATIVITY • MASTERY • ENERGY • AWARENESS • INSPIRATION • EMPOWERMENT • INITIATIVE

Celtic Cross Positions

1. **SIGNIFICATOR:** You have a strong will and can turn ideas into reality. Skilled at adapting to changing circumstances and juggling ideas.

2. **OBSTACLES:** You might be so focused that you ignore your intuition and deeper needs.

3. **ROOT:** Things are in motion. All you can do now is watch the situation unfold.

4. **PAST:** You recently invested time and energy into creating something or learning a new skill.

5. **CROWN:** An opportunity to change your situation. It is a time of coming into your own and creating something to be proud of.

6. **NEAR FUTURE:** You will likely be successful if you put hard work, study and energy into future plans and projects.

7. **FEAR:** You fear losing control or being under the influence of others. It may represent a persuasive or manipulative person.

8. **JUDGEMENT:** Others view you as skilful in your field. You seem to have the wisdom and skills to turn ideas into reality.

9. **HOPE:** A desire to manipulate a situation, alter a course or change direction. You may hope that you can make something happen if you focus enough energy into it.

10. **OUTCOME:** A time of action. You can realise your dreams if you invest time and energy. You can make a difference using the skills you have mastered. You have the ability to communicate, persuade, create or invent. Don't allow self-doubt to creep in.

OPPOSING CARDS

THE HIGH PRIESTESS
intuition, inaction, the unconscious

THE HANGED MAN
suspending action, not doing

SEVEN OF CUPS
lacking focus, lacking commitment

FOUR OF SWORDS
resting quietly, storing energy

REINFORCING CARDS

THE CHARIOT
focus, concentration, being forceful

TWO OF WANDS
personal power, wielding a strong force

EIGHT OF WANDS
quick action, making your move

THREE OF PENTACLES
skills, learning, apprenticeship

EIGHT OF PENTACLES
focus, concentration

• SPIRITUALITY • DREAMS • ILLUMINATION • AWAKENING • THE UNCONSCIOUS • SECRETS

2 The High Priestess

The High Priestess represents a time for meditation, inner discovery and reflection, not physical action. This card encourages you to look beyond the material realm, trust your intuition, and seek spiritual guidance. She symbolises the unknown. Pay attention to your dreams and subconscious if she appears in a reading.

DESCRIPTION
The High Priestess wears a crown of a full moon resting between a waxing and a waning moon. She sits between a black pillar (Boaz) and a white pillar (Jachin), representing the forces that maintain life. Hidden between them is the unconscious mind, dreams, and the mysteries of life. She holds a scroll inscribed with TORA, representing religious law. Behind her is a veil with palm trees and pomegranates – male and female symbols of reproduction. On the ground lies a crescent moon.

OVERVIEW
The High Priestess encourages you to look for omens along your path. If you must make a decision, this card advises you to trust your instincts and intuition. This card also suggests that a secret will be revealed.

LOVE
If you are in a relationship, The High Priestess hints that secrets exist between you and your partner. If you are single, this card warns against becoming involved with an emotionally withdrawn person.

CAREER
The High Priestess suggests there may be secrets at work – either you or a colleague are being dishonest. Try to solve the current problem using your intuition. This is an excellent time to think about your future career plans and goals, but not a time to take action.

SPIRITUALITY
The High Priestess indicates that you need to trust your intuition and instincts. It may also be encouraging you to study a spiritual discipline.

ADVICE
Pay more attention to your deeper feelings. If you have been detached from yourself lately, this card suggests you need to reconnect.

• INNER WISDOM • PSYCHIC ABILITY • INTUITION • INACTION • MYSTERY • HIDDEN EMOTIONS

Celtic Cross Positions

1. **SIGNIFICATOR:** You are mysterious, sensitive and intuitive. You may desire to connect with someone who seeks deeper meaning or you are seeking this deeper meaning yourself.

2. **OBSTACLES:** Hidden influences, possible secrets. A woman's influence, intuition or the unconscious.

3. **ROOT:** Your current situation possibly stems from your creative side. A period of tapping into undeveloped potential. It may represent a woman who is difficult to understand.

4. **PAST:** A recent event where you followed your intuition and based your actions on unconscious influences. It can also imply a secret that affects the current situation. Perhaps the answer you seek has already been revealed – someone may have dropped a clue in a recent conversation.

5. **CROWN:** Subtle influences from the unconscious are guiding you. Tap into inner resources for creativity or intuition. It may indicate meeting an aloof or spiritual woman.

6. **NEAR FUTURE:** The power of the feminine. Intuition, creativity or insight will play a role. The ability to tap into undeveloped potential. A remembered conversation may lead to the answers you are seeking. Rely on your intuition for guidance.

7. **FEAR:** Indicates a fear of your feminine side or your creative, intuitive, psychic and sensitive aspects.

8. **JUDGEMENT:** Others view you as spiritual or intuitive. Having the wisdom of an old soul. It represents a quiet person who appears to be secretive.

9. **HOPE:** You desire to follow your intuition or you wish to meet someone in tune with the unconscious world.

10. **OUTCOME:** A period of acknowledging your intuition and creative powers. You may discover a secret. You could soon be enlightened about a problem. A time for inward exploration and personal growth.

OPPOSING CARDS

THE MAGICIAN
acting consciously, thinking, the known

TWO OF WANDS
acting boldly

SEVEN OF WANDS
being aggressive

EIGHT OF WANDS
putting plans into action

REINFORCING CARDS

THE HERMIT
looking inwards, withdrawing, seeking guidance

THE HANGED MAN
suspended activity, waiting

FOUR OF SWORDS
resting quietly, contemplating

• MOTHERHOOD • CREATIVITY • PREGNANCY • SENSUALITY • ABUNDANCE • HEALING • NURTURING

3 The Empress

The Empress embodies motherhood. She is kind, loving and nurturing. The Empress also symbolises fertility and giving birth — either to a child, relationship, idea or project. You are likely to be feeling creative when this card arrives in your reading.

OVERVIEW
The Empress represents femininity and motherhood. She encourages you to fully commit to whatever you choose to do. Now is a good time to start a project as The Empress promises success. You may be required to mother someone or allow someone to mother you through a tricky time. This card can also indicate moving into a new home.

LOVE
The Empress is a positive card in a relationship spread, as she suggests an upcoming commitment, such as marriage. Pregnancy is also a possibility. If you are single, The Empress suggests you might soon enter a new relationship.

CAREER
With The Empress in a career spread, you are likely to be feeling creative and full of ideas. She tells you that now is an excellent time to start a new venture or project.

SPIRITUALITY
Spending time in nature may help you to reconnect with your spiritual side.

ADVICE
This card might be advising you to take on a mothering role in your relationship in order to motivate your partner.

DESCRIPTION
The Empress sits at the edge of a field. Her clothing is decorated with pomegranates, symbolising fertility. There are 12 stars on her crown, representing the 12 months and the 12 zodiac signs. She holds a sceptre topped with a globe. To her right is a heart-shaped shield engraved with the symbol of Venus (sexuality, birth and happiness). Behind her is a forest. The waterfall represents the flow of the unconscious into the conscious.

• FERTILITY • PASSION • CHILDBIRTH • MARRIAGE • PROSPERITY • NATURE • MATERNAL

Celtic Cross Positions

1. **SIGNIFICATOR:** You are creative, nurturing and loving. Possibly interested in horticulture, art, music or design. Material security is crucial to you.

2. **OBSTACLES:** You need to find a way to balance your own needs with the responsibilities of a relationship or parenthood.

3. **ROOT:** Your love for family forms the base of all your decisions.

4. **PAST:** A recent time of material comforts, successful projects and abundance. You might have just moved home.

5. **CROWN:** Indicates material comforts, meeting an earthy woman, or an opportunity for growth or expansion.

6. **NEAR FUTURE:** Represents the development of relationships, possible marriage or pregnancy. It suggests abundance and well-being. Indicates the development and fruition of projects.

7. **FEAR:** You fear marriage, pregnancy or parenthood.

8. **JUDGEMENT:** Represents a highly confident, well-balanced individual who can be relied on.

9. **HOPE:** You may desire material comforts, a new home, marriage, pregnancy, a family or productivity.

10. **OUTCOME:** Represents loving and being loved. It indicates a solid relationship and home life. Abundance, fruitfulness and fertility. A period of satisfaction, pleasure and contentment. A good time to start a creative project.

OPPOSING CARDS

THE EMPEROR
fathering, order and discipline, regularity

DEATH
principal of death

FOUR OF PENTACLES
miserly, possessiveness

NINE OF PENTACLES
refinement, sophistication

REINFORCING CARDS

THE LOVERS
sexual fulfilment, pleasure

THE STAR
generosity, free-flowing love

NINE OF CUPS
enjoying the senses

SEVEN OF PENTACLES
material reward

TEN OF PENTACLES
affluence, luxury, physical comfort

• POWER • FINANCIAL SECURITY • LEADERSHIP • AUTHORITY • RESPONSIBILITY • ORDER

4 The Emperor

The Emperor is a powerful figure who embodies logic, reason and accomplishment. When this card appears in a reading, it indicates an excellent time to take charge and build a career. The Emperor does not seek conflict but is unafraid to stand his ground.

OVERVIEW
The Emperor is solid and stable, but can be rigid and stubborn. This card signifies the dominance of logic over emotion. It can indicate that you have more power than you think and that it is time to believe in yourself. You may need to stand up for your beliefs and put your foot down. It may mean that someone with The Emperor's qualities will enter your life.

LOVE
For those in a relationship, this card is a good sign that things will get serious. If you are single, this card can indicate a romantic relationship with someone who embodies the characteristics of The Emperor.

CAREER
The Emperor is an auspicious card in a career reading, suggesting authority and success. Good opportunities are coming, you should have success with job hunting or promotion. An older colleague may offer guidance.

SPIRITUALITY
The Emperor suggests that now is a time to be more structured in your spiritual approach.

ADVICE
Don't be afraid to stand up for yourself but don't get emotional. Act calmly and speak with clarity.

DESCRIPTION
The Emperor sits on a stone throne engraved with rams' heads, symbolising the planet Mars and the zodiac sign Aries, which represents courage and leadership. He wears a suit of armour under his cloak, showing that he is ready to battle if necessary. He wears a crown and holds the sceptre of Ankh (symbol of eternal life) and a golden globe. The landscape behind him suggests that hard decisions might be required. He is paired with The Empress. He symbolises power and authority.

• PROTECTOR • FATHERHOOD • STRUCTURE • REGULATION • PRACTICAL • CONTROL • BOUNDARIES

Celtic Cross Positions

1. **SIGNIFICATOR:** You are authoritative, influential and have good leadership qualities. Intelligent and responsible, dependable and practical.

2. **OBSTACLES:** Represents authority and responsibility. The situation is under control.

3. **ROOT:** Stability, strong decision-making skills, an established foundation. A person of authority, power and control. Building towards success.

4. **PAST:** An authoritative and protective figure has a bearing on the situation. Being focused on security or control has perhaps led you to this point. Suggests you are carrying a heavy burden.

5. **CROWN:** You are moving into a period of stability. Creating foundations for the future. A person in authority might be hindering your progress.

6. **NEAR FUTURE:** Represents a secure time of structure, stability and control. It suggests a possible paternity or responsibility. It indicates establishing foundations of support. You may be seeking permanency or protection.

7. **FEAR:** A fear of authority, responsibility, paternity or being locked into something.

8. **JUDGEMENT:** Represents a powerful individual. A good provider who is courageous, trustworthy, stable and protective.

9. **HOPE:** You hope for authority and stability. A desire for a family or financial security.

10. **OUTCOME:** Represents a time of material success and financial security. You may need to stand up for your beliefs or protect someone who relies on you. If you approach issues in a rational way, success is likely to be yours.

OPPOSING CARDS

THE EMPRESS
mothering, abundance

SEVEN OF CUPS
dissipating, lack of order

FIVE OF SWORDS
bending the rules, breaking the law

REINFORCING CARDS

THE HIEROPHANT
conforming to rules

JUSTICE
concerns of justice, legalities

TWO OF WANDS
having authority

THREE OF WANDS
assuming leadership

FOUR OF PENTACLES
control, structure, order

• ORTHODOX • CONFORMITY • RELIGION • RITUAL • TRADITION • SPIRITUAL FOUNDATIONS • MORALITY

5 The Hierophant

The Hierophant symbolises rules, regulations and orthodox thinking. This card has two primary meanings – the search for spiritual depth or the benefit of being conventional. It also refers to giving or receiving wise counsel.

OVERVIEW
The Hierophant symbolises traditional values, ceremonies and organised religion. It also represents someone who is narrow-minded and very set in their ways. It might be time to accept conventional behaviour and not rock the boat. This card hints at legal procedures.

LOVE
The Hierophant indicates the legal aspects of relationships, such as marriage contracts. If you are currently having relationship difficulties, this card suggests a conventional solution. If you are single, perhaps your desire for a deep commitment is preventing you from finding it.

CAREER
The Hierophant suggests success if you follow traditional, conventional methods. This is a good time to study. Either you or someone else may be called upon to offer advice. The card may also point to legal issues and contracts.

SPIRITUALITY
The Hierophant suggests that you are looking for answers within. A spiritual advisor might be coming into your life.

ADVICE
Are you too stuck in your ways and unwilling to evolve and adapt? Try to be a bit more flexible and understanding of those who are different to you.

DESCRIPTION
The Hierophant sits between two pillars (similar to The High Priestess), representing freedom and conformity or law. His three-tiered crown represents the body, mind and spirit. The triple cross represents his ability to merge the material, physical and spiritual. Two fingers point to the sky and two point towards the Earth. Two priests, one wearing red roses (desire) and the other white lilies (purity/spiritual thought), await his blessing and advice.

• INDOCTRINATION • EDUCATION • BELIEF SYSTEMS • SOCIAL GROUP • FAITH

Celtic Cross Positions

1. **SIGNIFICATOR:** You are steady, reliable and orthodox. Perhaps a teacher, counsellor or priest. Conscious awareness of community and a moral understanding of right and wrong.

2. **OBSTACLES:** You are feeling the forces of convention. Being pulled towards approval, conformity or religious acceptance.

3. **ROOT:** Represents conforming to social conventions. Seeking religious or spiritual guidance.

4. **PAST:** A time of conformity, religious instruction or counselling. Perhaps you previously searched for answers through religion. A time when you looked to others for solutions, approval or were swayed by peer pressure.

5. **CROWN:** Imposing structure and meaning on a situation. Concern over how your lifestyle and desires conform to social expectations. Seeking approval for past or present actions.

6. **NEAR FUTURE:** Seeking comfort in the familiar and keeping with tradition. Following the path of least resistance. Looking to religion for solace and guidance.

7. **FEAR:** You desire to stand out and break free from convention and expectations.

8. **JUDGEMENT:** You seek approval and adhere rigidly to social norms. You are very stuck in your ways and have a clear moral compass.

9. **HOPE:** Represents hope to find wisdom and answers through religion. A longing to find spiritual meaning in practical affairs. It also indicates a desire to stick with what you know is steadfast and true.

10. **OUTCOME:** Represents finding solace and answers through religion, counselling or social structures. Indicates indoctrination or institutional beliefs. Also conventional ways of approaching things. You may meet a spiritual advisor who has positive guidance for you.

OPPOSING CARDS

THE FOOL
being crazy, unorthodox

THE LOVERS
personal beliefs

TWO OF WANDS
a pioneer, diverging from the crowd

SEVEN OF SWORDS
being a lone wolf

TWO OF PENTACLES
being flexible, changing with the times

REINFORCING CARDS

THE EMPEROR
following the rules

THREE OF CUPS
focusing on the group

EIGHT OF PENTACLES
learning, studying

TEN OF PENTACLES
conforming, following the rules, conservative

• LOVE • MARRIAGE • ATTRACTION • COMMITMENT • TEMPTATION • RELATIONSHIPS • ROMANCE

6 The Lovers

The Lovers symbolises the power of love and union. It is also a card about choices and their consequences. Its presence in a reading indicates that you will soon be faced with an important choice.

DESCRIPTION
A naked couple stand in a garden. An angel is in the sky with outstretched arms. The man looks at the woman as she gazes at the angel. In the Tree of Knowledge behind the woman is a snake who whispers in her ear.
The Tree of Life grows behind the man with twelve fiery leaves. The two trees symbolise opposites (male and female, good and evil, unconscious and conscious desires).

OVERVIEW
The Lovers can refer to a fulfilling, meaningful relationship based on trust and deep connection. This card is a reminder that you cannot give yourself fully in love without understanding your own beliefs and values. It also represents making a choice which often involves sacrifice. You may have to choose between two lovers or be faced with a different type of decision that will have far-reaching effects.

LOVE
In a relationship reading, the Lovers signifies love, kindred spirits and a deep bond. If you have just met someone, this card hints that the relationship might become meaningful. However, whether you are single or in a relationship, the Lovers can also represent having to choose between two partners.

CAREER
The Lovers represents partnerships and trust in a career context. There might be romance brewing in the office. You might also be faced with an important decision at work.

SPIRITUALITY
Spiritually, this card indicates finding personal happiness within yourself, discovering who you are, and what matters to you.

ADVICE
Make sure you aren't in love with the idea of being in love or you might be using love to escape confronting yourself.

• PERSONAL BELIEFS • SURRENDER • UNITY • PARTNERSHIPS • FRIENDSHIPS • CHOICE • FULFILMENT

Celtic Cross Positions

1. **SIGNIFICATOR:** You are easily tempted – whether by beauty, love, romance or sexuality. You might be preoccupied with a choice that lies ahead.

2. **OBSTACLES:** Represents sexual attraction, temptation and choice.

3. **ROOT:** Your choices have led you to this situation. You might be regretting them.

4. **PAST:** Thoughts of a previous relationship are preoccupying you.

5. **CROWN:** You may be contemplating a choice or whether to give into temptation.

6. **NEAR FUTURE:** An important decision needs to be made. It also represents a new relationship, commitment, engagement or marriage.

7. **FEAR:** You fear emotional involvement or being responsible for someone else. It can also indicate being scared of making the wrong choice.

8. **JUDGEMENT:** Represents an individual easily tempted by romance. Or someone who finds it difficult to make decisions.

9. **HOPE:** Represents hope for romance or a meaningful relationship, commitment or marriage. It may indicate a wish to find your soulmate.

10. **OUTCOME:** A choice needs to be made between two equally desirable options. Can also suggest a relationship that meets both your physical and spiritual needs. Commitment or marriage, or a choice between physical desire and spiritual love. The union of soulmates.

OPPOSING CARDS

THE HIEROPHANT
group beliefs

THE HERMIT
being alone, not relating, less sexual

FIVE OF CUPS
loss of friendships

THREE OF SWORDS
rejection, separation

SIX OF SWORDS
toil, hardship

REINFORCING CARDS

TWO OF CUPS
sexual fulfilment, pleasure

NINE OF CUPS
sexual pleasure

TEN OF CUPS
family relationships, bonding

TEN OF PENTACLES
family ties, permanent unions

• CONQUEST • WILLPOWER • STRUGGLE • TRIUMPH • GOALS • AMBITION • VICTORY • TRAVEL

7 The Chariot

The Chariot symbolises overcoming challenges by using willpower and focus. It encourages self-reliance and harnessing your emotions. It can also indicate business-related travel.

OVERVIEW
The Chariot represents successfully overcoming obstacles and not allowing emotions to sway you. Pay attention to what lies ahead and keep your focus. The Chariot can also suggest that you are being pulled in two directions and may need to stand your ground. This card can also represent travel.

LOVE
If you are in a relationship, The Chariot advises you to be practical. If there are issues, it suggests that these might be overcome. If you are single, The Chariot indicates that you should focus on yourself for the time being and not get emotionally involved.

CAREER
In a work context, The Chariot suggests that you are feeling motivated and ambitious. If you have plans and goals, keep focused and work towards them. Travel is also indicated. If there has been conflict at work, this card suggests that the issues will be sorted out quickly if emotions are kept in check.

SPIRITUALITY
The Chariot can represent a spiritual journey.

ADVICE
If it feels like you are being pulled in two directions, take some time to decide what you want before making your choice.

DESCRIPTION
A prince stands in a chariot, pulled by two sphinxes representing opposing negative and positive forces. He controls his urges by willpower, represented by his wand. The square on his chest symbolises Earth, balance and strength. The star on his crown symbolises strength and illumination. Above him is a blue canopy decorated with white stars indicating celestial influences. The winged shield, lifted by the wings of a golden globe, displays the Hindu lingam-yoni (symbolising creation and regeneration).

• SELF-CONTROL • POWER • JOURNEY • DISCIPLINE • SUCCESS • SELF-ASSERTIVE • HARD CONTROL

Celtic Cross Positions

1. **SIGNIFICATOR:** You are self-confident, disciplined and ambitious. Extremely passionate with strong willpower.

2. **OBSTACLES:** Represents focus, willpower, determination and the ability to resist temptation.

3. **ROOT:** You are disciplined and have a keen sense of direction. You are currently striving against all odds to reach a goal. You know what you want and how to get it.

4. **PAST:** Represents past success through willpower, focus and control. Perhaps a significant journey which affects this reading.

5. **CROWN:** You desire to win and are pursuing your goal with full force.

6. **NEAR FUTURE:** Represents victory, achieving a goal and being filled with confidence or ambition. It also indicates movement and travel.

7. **FEAR:** You are scared to change where you are, afraid of losing control. Lack of self-confidence and fear of failure keep you immobile.

8. **JUDGEMENT:** This represents someone who appears determined and driven to the point of never giving up, no matter the cost. It indicates someone who is always on top of things.

9. **HOPE:** You wish to have success and achieve your goals. You may also want to leave town or take a holiday.

10. **OUTCOME:** Success is likely if you focus on the current project. You have the ability to rise above any problems that arise. Take control, master your emotions and forge the way forward. It also suggests a journey.

OPPOSING CARDS

STRENGTH
soft control

THE HANGED MAN
accepting fate, putting others first

THE TOWER
accepting defeat, humbling oneself

EIGHT OF SWORDS
self-doubt confusion

TEN OF SWORDS
defeat, powerless, putting others first

REINFORCING CARDS

THE MAGICIAN
using your will, concentrating

TWO OF WANDS
being in authority, dominating

SIX OF WANDS
triumph, self-control

FOUR OF PENTACLES
control

NINE OF PENTACLES
self-control, discipline

• INNER STRENGTH • PATIENCE • CALM • DETERMINATION • SOFT CONTROL • HARMONY

8 Strength

DESCRIPTION
Calmly, and with her bare hands, a woman in white holds back the King of Beasts. The white robe and the flowers in her hair symbolise purity. The figure 8 above her head is a sign of eternity. It represents the balancing of opposing forces. The woman is calm yet focused. She displays no fear.

When Strength appears in your spread, a subtle approach is called for. Strength is similar to a trickling brook that, over time, carves out the land through patience and determination. Strength advocates virtue over vice and a calm yet forceful approach.

OVERVIEW
A challenging time might lie ahead, and you are advised to master your emotions and approach the issue calmly. This card suggests that the situation might not be as difficult as you imagine. Strength reminds us of the importance of the right attitude and taking things step by step. Strength also suggests that positive encouragement and kindness can tame someone's wild nature.

LOVE
If you are in a relationship, Strength indicates a healthy partnership that benefits both of you. If you are single, this card suggests you might meet a loving and calm person.

CAREER
Strength is a positive career card. It advises you to master your emotions and believe in yourself. You have the ability, skills and potential to be successful. Resist emotional outbursts or the use of undue force.

SPIRITUALITY
In a spiritual context, Strength suggests that you are feeling strongly connected to your deeper self.

ADVICE
Take a calm approach to the anger of others. You can be assertive without being nasty.

• COURAGE • FORTITUDE • SELF-AWARENESS • DISCIPLINE • PERSEVERANCE • FAITH • COMPASSION

Celtic Cross Positions

1. **SIGNIFICATOR:** You are self-aware and courageous. You have a big heart and strong willpower.

2. **OBSTACLES:** Represents inner or spiritual strength, the courage to act alone.

3. **ROOT:** You have the inner strength, faith and determination that you need to overcome this.

4. **PAST:** A time when you were steadfast and confident, or when your sense of conviction was unwavering. Perhaps you resisted temptation or overcame obstacles. A time you think back on with pride.

5. **CROWN:** Represents having faith in yourself and your beliefs. It suggests using inner strength and willpower to disarm negativity.

6. **NEAR FUTURE:** To overcome the issue, you must have faith in yourself. You will find the inner strength and willpower to do what needs to be done. Strength suggests that you will overcome temptation or adversity.

7. **FEAR:** You fear not finding the inner strength that you need. A fear of losing control.

8. **JUDGEMENT:** Represents someone strong and confident who can be counted on for support. A person with a balanced personality.

9. **HOPE:** A desire for courage in the face of temptation, hoping for self-control.

10. **OUTCOME:** Represents an upcoming challenge. You will be successful if you maintain mastery over your emotions. Be prepared to stand your ground.

OPPOSING CARDS

EIGHT OF CUPS
weariness, feeling weak

SIX OF SWORDS
being listless, lacking heart

FIVE OF PENTACLES
ill health, weakness

REINFORCING CARDS

THE HANGED MAN
taking time, patience

NINE OF WANDS
stamina, strength to endure

• KNOWLEDGE • DISCRETION • SILENCE • SEARCH FOR TRUTH • INWARD JOURNEY • INTROSPECTION

9 The Hermit

The Hermit's appearance in a spread indicates that you need to spend some time alone. It symbolises the power of solitude and spending time with ourselves. This card encourages thinking things through before acting.

DESCRIPTION
A bearded man stands alone on a snow-capped mountain. The sky is calm and clear. He holds a staff in his right hand while looking down at the path he has travelled. His lantern lights the way of truth. Both the lantern and staff are symbolic tools of his journey. The landscape shows that he is truly alone and isolated.

OVERVIEW
The Hermit can indicate a time of wonderful self-analyses and getting in touch with your inner guide. You may meet a teacher or spiritual guru who will offer advice, or you may need to turn to your inner guide for answers. This card advises you not to make important decisions now. It is time to withdraw and find peace in solitude.

LOVE
If you are in a relationship, The Hermit suggests you should not make a long-term commitment at the moment. If you are single, this card represents a period of being alone.

CAREER
The Hermit is not a strong career card. It advises that you refrain from making important decisions and act with integrity. You may receive advice from an older, wiser colleague.

SPIRITUALITY
In a spiritual reading, The Hermit encourages you to take an inward journey and get to know your spirit guide. Spend time meditating or walking alone in nature.

ADVICE
While it is important to be alone right now, don't consciously push people away.

· REFLECTION · SEARCHING · SOLITUDE · CONTEMPLATION · WITHDRAWAL · GUIDANCE · CAUTION

Celtic Cross Positions

1. **SIGNIFICATOR:** You use insight and knowledge to seek the truth. A confident teacher, counsellor or spiritual guide.

2. **OBSTACLES:** A physical withdrawal from a situation. Preparation and patience before action.

3. **ROOT:** A spiritual or intellectual journey. Believe in yourself and your inner wisdom. It may indicate wise counsel or a spiritual guide.

4. **PAST:** You recently withdrew from society and spent time in solitude, meditation and introspection.

5. **CROWN:** An opportunity for personal growth. Independence, a period of solitude or withdrawal. A teacher or guide may be coming into your life.

6. **NEAR FUTURE:** A decision to spend time in the internal world. It suggests seeking a path to enlightenment, seeking to understand yourself. It may also indicate a teacher or guide.

7. **FEAR:** You fear being alone or isolated. It can also suggest a fear of old age.

8. **JUDGEMENT:** An independent thinker who relies upon inner strength and wisdom.

9. **HOPE:** You desire to find answers through time spent alone. You may be hoping to make time for yourself, or to distance yourself from a situation. A desire for solitude or independence.

10. **OUTCOME:** Represents seeking wisdom and knowledge through independence or introspection. It suggests a period of silence and solitude for reflection and mediation.

OPPOSING CARDS

THE LOVERS
being in a relationship, sexuality

THE WORLD
involvement with the world, engaging

TWO OF CUPS
partnerships, making connections

THREE OF CUPS
being in a group, being with others

JUSTICE
facing consequences

REINFORCING CARDS

THE HIGH PRIESTESS
looking inward, withdrawing

FOUR OF CUPS
withdrawing, introverted

EIGHT OF CUPS
searching for deeper meaning

FOUR OF SWORDS
contemplating, being still and quiet

SEVEN OF SWORDS
being alone, staying away from others

• DESTINY • CHANGE • LETTING GO • TURNING POINT • MOVEMENT • COMPLETION • PERSONAL VISION

10 Wheel of Fortune

The Wheel of Fortune indicates that change is on the horizon. A cycle has ended and a new one is about to begin. Considered to be auspicious, this card indicates that destiny is involved.

OVERVIEW
The Wheel of Fortune indicates that things are about to change, usually for the better. Current difficulties may soon be resolved. Whether the wheel spins in your favour is currently out of your control. You might be called upon to pay for past actions. Many outside events affect our lives, and karma often plays a role.

LOVE
In love, The Wheel of Fortune usually indicates a change for the better. You may meet someone new, find ways to improve an existing relationship or break away from an unhappy relationship.

CAREER
In a career context, this card is usually a good omen which encourages you to follow your dreams.

SPIRITUALITY
The Wheel of Fortune indicates that your destiny is leading you. Watch for signs and omens along your path and seize opportunities offered.

ADVICE
You might feel disillusioned and believe you have no control over your life. The Wheel of Fortune can make you feel powerless, but it is your choices that help it to spin. Your destiny is woven into it.

DESCRIPTION
The wheel has two circles, one inside the other. The centre circle has symbols representing the four elements. Depending on which way you read it, the outer circle says TORA, TARO or ROTA (Latin for wheel), interspersed with the Hebrew letters YHWH. On top sits a sphinx holding the Sword of Destiny. The snake represents the Egyptian God Typhon, and the jackal-headed is the Egyptian God Anubis. In each corner is a winged creature – a lion, a bull, an eagle and an angel (Leo, Taurus, Aquarius and Scorpio).

• PROGRESS • CHANGE OF FORTUNE • FATE • OPPORTUNITIES • KARMA • CHOICES • BALANCE • NEW CYCLE

Celtic Cross Positions

1. **SIGNIFICATOR:** Situations and events in your life are as they should be. What is happening needs to happen.

2. **OBSTACLES:** Represents a change of fortune. Natural forces are pulling in a different direction. Karma and destiny.

3. **ROOT:** Represents the natural course of events on a destined path. One thing leads to another as if by coincidence.

4. **PAST:** A past event when you had a change in fortune or circumstance. Perhaps this period of good luck has ended.

5. **CROWN:** A change in fate or the beginning of a new cycle. A window of opportunity.

6. **NEAR FUTURE:** Represents a shift in fate or luck. The time for change is coming. New opportunities are on the horizon. The beginning of a new cycle.

7. **FEAR:** You fear change and are worried that your luck is running out. A fear of what is coming.

8. **JUDGEMENT:** Someone who accepts fate and makes the best of it. It may suggest a person who always seems to have good luck.

9. **HOPE:** You are hoping for a change in fortune. Wishing for an end or a beginning.

10. **OUTCOME:** Represents a change of fortune. It indicates new opportunities. Doors opening, options and choices, a new cycle or phase. It suggests a period of good luck and unexpected success.

OPPOSING CARDS

TWO OF SWORDS
being stuck, at an impasse

FOUR OF SWORDS
rest, quiet, slow pace

FOUR OF PENTACLES
blocked change, no movement

SEVEN OF PENTACLES
assessment before direction of change

REINFORCING CARDS

EIGHT OF WANDS
rapid pace, quick developments

· JUSTICE · RESPONSIBILITY · DECISIONS · CAUSE AND EFFECT · BALANCED HARMONY · KARMA · TRIAL

11 Justice

DESCRIPTION
Justice wears a red robe and a green cloak. She sits between two pillars representing the opposing forces of right and wrong, addition and subtraction, reward and punishment. Her cloak is fastened with a square brooch, symbolising the Earth and balance. Her three-pronged crown represents balance and harmony. She holds a double-edged sword and the golden scales of balanced judgement. Behind her hangs a purple veil of wisdom.

Justice is a very clear-cut card. Things are either right or wrong, there is no in-between area. Justice does not allow emotions to affect decision making and can be brutal. Justice warns that you will be held accountable for past actions.

OVERVIEW
Justice is a reminder that actions have consequences and stresses the importance of fairness and balance. If a decision needs to be made, Justice advises you to be objective. You may need to accept certain truths about yourself and listen to the viewpoints of others. Justice can also indicate legal issues and disputes but suggests a fair outcome.

LOVE
If you are in a relationship, Justice recommends that you act in a fair manner and are truthful. You may need to make a decision which does not include your partner.

CAREER
In a career reading, this card stresses the importance of balancing your work and personal life. Justice tells you that you'll get what you deserve. If you have been underhanded, you may need to pay for this soon. If you have been fair, balanced and honest in your dealings, Justice suggests that you'll receive rewards.

SPIRITUALITY
In a spiritual context, Justice advises you to stay grounded. It encourages you to look for the truth and accept the consequences of your actions.

ADVICE
No one likes a know-it-all. You might feel very sure of your situation and opinion, but it won't hurt to listen to the viewpoints of others. Perhaps there is something important that you have overlooked?

• PARTNERSHIPS • LEGAL MATTERS • INCORRUPTIBILITY • FAIRNESS • CHOICE • JUDGEMENT • CLARITY

Celtic Cross Positions

1. **SIGNIFICATOR:** You have a strong moral code and desire harmony and peace. It also can mean litigation. It may indicate a lawyer or philanthropist.

2. **OBSTACLES:** You are distracted by a possible lawsuit or legal action. It suggests a fair and just outcome.

3. **ROOT:** Represents a search for answers, seeking the truth. Decision-making or litigation.

4. **PAST:** You recently got what you deserved, positive or negative, based on your actions. You need to accept this and move on. It can also suggest that legal contracts have recently been signed or fair agreements have been reached.

5. **CROWN:** Solutions will soon become apparent. A pending settlement or judgement. It suggests fairness.

6. **NEAR FUTURE:** Justice and favourable judgements. You may require legal contracts. It indicates positive and fair outcomes.

7. **FEAR:** You fear a lawsuit, legal action or contracts. A fear of a decision outside of your control.

8. **JUDGEMENT:** Represents a balanced person who understands the meaning of fairness and strives to uphold it.

9. **HOPE:** Hope for a fair and positive outcome. Wishing for a favourable judgement, legal action or lawsuit.

10. **OUTCOME:** Represents positive outcomes with fair and impartial judgements. It suggests seeking solutions, fairness or truth. It indicates a rational decision or situation. On another level, it suggests legalities.

OPPOSING CARDS

TWO OF SWORDS
avoiding the truth, precarious balance

FIVE OF SWORDS
lack of integrity, not doing what is right

SEVEN OF SWORDS
shirking responsibility

THE HERMIT
hiding from responsibilities

REINFORCING CARDS

THE EMPEROR
justice, regulations, legal issues

JUDGEMENT
deciding, accepting responsibility

NINE OF SWORDS
realising mistakes, guilt over the past

TEN OF SWORDS
accepting responsibility, being accountable

SEVEN OF PENTACLES
deciding a future course, assessing where you are

WAITING • LETTING GO • SUSPENSION • PEACE • REVERSAL • SPIRITUAL CLEANSING • NEW PERSPECTIVE

12 The Hanged Man

The Hanged Man symbolises a moment of pause. It could indicate a time when nothing seems to happen. It might also be warning that you may need to sacrifice something in order to move forward.

OVERVIEW
The Hanged Man often appears when life is going through a slump. A period between two phases, where things are not yet aligned. It is not the time for action. The Hanged Man tells you to accept the situation and not to rock the boat or force the issue. Make peace with the pause. It might also imply that a sacrifice is necessary for growth.

LOVE
The Hanged Man can imply that your relationship is stagnating or that you are waiting for your partner to make a decision. If you are single, The Hanged Man suggests that you should relax, let go and let things unfold without trying to dictate the outcome.

CAREER
The Hanged Man indicates a pause between jobs or feeling unsure about the future. It is not the time for decisions that may have long-term repercussions. You may need to make a sacrifice in order to move forward.

SPIRITUALITY
You might need to give something up to evolve spiritually. It is a time of introspection, surrender and meditation.

ADVICE
This might feel like a frustrating time, especially if you are used to high action. But this pause is crucial – as one phase ends, we need to stop and reflect before the next phase begins, and let go of emotional baggage.

DESCRIPTION
A young man with a golden nimbus hangs upside down by his right foot from a gallows tree, which forms a Tau cross. The man's left leg intersects and falls behind his right, creating a fylfot cross. His arms are behind his back. His elbows are out to the side form an inverted triangle with his head, representing water and the unconscious. He appears calm and at peace with the situation.

• SURRENDER • SPIRITUAL GROWTH • SACRIFICE • BREAK FROM PAST • TRANSITION • PATIENCE

Celtic Cross Positions

1. **SIGNIFICATOR:** You are currently not in control. You need to surrender and wait patiently. A social worker, a writer, an actor, a therapist or a psychologist.

2. **OBSTACLES:** Change, awkwardness, surrender, sacrifice. It can also suggest that you are ignoring the past.

3. **ROOT:** Try to approach the situation from another angle to get a new perspective.

4. **PAST:** Suggests a recent time when you relinquished control, gave up or let others take charge. A time when you were unable to make decisions. This still has influence on the current situation.

5. **CROWN:** Indecision, closing all doors and avenues for retreat. Backing yourself into a corner. It suggests an inability to act.

6. **NEAR FUTURE:** A conscious decision to give up or surrender something for a good reason. It may indicate a period of inaction.

7. **FEAR:** You fear being restrained and unable to take action. A fear of the repercussions caused by changing your mind. A fear of sacrifice.

8. **JUDGEMENT:** Someone who can't make up their mind or someone willing to sacrifice for a good cause.

9. **HOPE:** A desire not to make decisions, or be taken advantage of. A wish for a successful outcome without having to give anything up.

10. **OUTCOME:** You may need to sacrifice something, either material or emotional. Perhaps you are at a crossroads and contemplating a completely different way of life. Re-evaluating a situation.

OPPOSING CARDS

THE MAGICIAN
action, doing, creating

THE CHARIOT
self assertion, determination, control

SEVEN OF WANDS
defiance, struggling against

TEN OF WANDS
struggle

FOUR OF PENTACLES
holding on, control

REINFORCING CARDS

THE FOOL
faith in what is, going with the flow

THE HIGH PRIESTESS
suspending activity, waiting

STRENGTH
patience, taking time out

FOUR OF SWORDS
rest, suspended activity

TEN OF SWORDS
sacrifice, martyrdom

• ENDING • CHANGE • TRANSITION • ELIMINATION • INEXORABLE FORCES • DEPARTURE

13 Death

Death does not predict actual death but suggests a massive change in your life. A time of passing from one phase to another.
The change can be external or internal. It can also refer to letting go of parts of yourself that no longer serve you.

OVERVIEW
Death signifies change and transformation. This can be a painful, sudden and traumatic experience which offers a chance to start over. It encourages you to embrace the new and let go of old habits and beliefs. This card hints at an exciting time ahead.

LOVE
If you are in a relationship, it might be ending or changing dramatically. If you are single, Death suggests that you need to undergo a transformation before committing to someone.

CAREER
Change and transformation are coming. Death is not a passive card, so if you want things to change, you will need to take action to move things along. Apply for that new position, study something that's always interested you, start a new venture. This card implies that it will likely be a change for the better.

SPIRITUALITY
Spiritual transformation is indicated, as well as change in your spiritual practice. This card can have long-lasting effects.

ADVICE
If the Death card scares you, perhaps you actually fear change and are concerned about the future. It can be challenging to let go and trust the process, but Death indicates that you should give it a go and embrace the changes.

DESCRIPTION
Death rides a white horse, the colour of purity and a symbol of strength and power. Death's skeleton represents the part of the body that survives death, and the armour shows invincibility. He carries a black flag decorated with a five-petal rose, reflecting beauty and immortality, and the number five represents change. These symbols reflect that death is about endings and beginnings, birth and rebirth.

• REBIRTH • END OF OLD • BEGINNING • DRASTIC CHANGE • TRANSFORMATION

Celtic Cross Positions

1. **SIGNIFICATOR:** You are going through a significant life transformation. The end of a negative period is at hand.

2. **OBSTACLES:** You are feeling the influences of a major transformation. The end of one thing and the beginning of another. A breakup or departure. Old habits, relationships and attitudes are phasing out of your life.

3. **ROOT:** Represents a drastic change. The ending of something has caused the present situation. You are passing from one stage to another.

4. **PAST:** You recently experienced a devastating loss or drastic change.

5. **CROWN:** On the verge of change and transformation. You are approaching the end of a situation, relationship, phase or cycle.

6. **NEAR FUTURE:** Represents drastic change. The end of a phase or situation. A departure from old ways.

7. **FEAR:** You fear transition, change or death.

8. **JUDGEMENT:** Represents someone who has given up hope. Someone who is grieving, depressed or enduring intense hardships.

9. **HOPE:** You hope for the current situation to end, a desire to leave the past behind you.

10. **OUTCOME:** Represents drastic change. A relationship, a situation, an event, or a way of life is ending. Embrace the changes coming – life will not be the same after this. A change for the positive.

OPPOSING CARDS

THE FOOL
beginning

THE EMPRESS
birth

JUDGEMENT
rebirth, fresh start

REINFORCING CARDS

THE CHARIOT
forceful, powerful movement

THE TOWER
sweeping impact, powerful forces

EIGHT OF WANDS
conclusion, ending

FIVE OF CUPS
loss, good-byes

EIGHT OF CUPS
moving on, finishing up

• TEMPERATE • BALANCED • HEALTH • COMBINING FORCES • POWER OF SUCCESS • CONTINUITY

14 Temperance

Temperance is self-controlled and careful. This card shows the power of blending things together to create harmony. It's a peaceful card which cautions against bad habits and excessive behaviour.

OVERVIEW
Temperance generally indicates the need for balance and warns against overdoing things. Peace, patience and moderation are the main influences. Temperance suggests that you slow down and find internal harmony and balance.

LOVE
If you are in a relationship, Temperance indicates that the relationship is well-balanced. If you are single, this card suggests that love can only enter your life when you have achieved inner balance and peace.

CAREER
Temperance encourages you to balance your work and personal life in order to achieve your goals. If there is conflict, it can be resolved through patience, understanding and moderation.

SPIRITUALITY
Spiritually, Temperance suggests meditating might be beneficial. This card also advises listening to your inner voice and trusting your intuition.

ADVICE
Do you lack self-control? Do you lash out at times and regret it afterwards? Temperance suggests that you need to learn balance and moderation if you want to be successful.

DESCRIPTION
An angel pours the contents of one chalice into another, showing the forces of the conscious and unconscious. Her robe has an orange triangle (symbolising upward aspirations) inside a white square (the Earth). The circle on her forehead suggests spiritual illumination. She stands with one foot on land and one foot in water, indicating the bridge between the conscious and the unconscious. The irises growing beside her symbolise a bridge between heaven and Earth.

• MODERATION • COMPROMISE • SELF-RESTRAINT • HARMONY • CALM • PEACE • VIRTUE

Celtic Cross Positions

1. **SIGNIFICATOR:** You have a balanced personality, great self-control, flexibility, and adaptability.

2. **OBSTACLES:** Your addictions and bad habits prevent you from moving forward. Develop self-control and restraint.

3. **ROOT:** Indicates choosing the middle path of moderation and compromise.

4. **PAST:** A time when you relied on mutual understanding and cooperation. Or when you were able to diffuse an argument using a calm approach.

5. **CROWN:** Represents introducing additional elements into your life or successfully balancing existing ones. Seeking compromise.

6. **NEAR FUTURE:** You may need to temper a volatile situation with a calm approach. Don't let the angry rising emotions of others affect your demeanour.

7. **FEAR:** You fear not being able to balance all of your responsibilities. A fear of poor management and limitations.

8. **JUDGEMENT:** Someone with well-balanced priorities and self-control. Someone good at resolving conflict.

9. **HOPE:** Represents a desire for harmony and balance in life.

10. **OUTCOME:** A time of cooperation, compromise and good relationships. A period of harmony and balance. This will be enhanced if you act with control and self-restraint. You may be required to resolve conflict.

OPPOSING CARDS

THE TOWER
extremes, exploding

FIVE OF WANDS
disagreement, competition, imbalance

SEVEN OF CUPS
excess, overindulgence

FIVE OF SWORDS
discord, lack of harmony

FIVE OF PENTACLES
ill health

REINFORCING CARDS

THE WORLD
integration, combination, synthesis

TWO OF CUPS
connection, working together

THREE OF CUPS
joining forces, working together

TWO OF PENTACLES
balancing, finding the right mix

THREE OF PENTACLES
team work, combining

• BONDAGE • MATERIALISM • TEMPTATION • IGNORANCE • HOPELESSNESS • SETTING BOUNDARIES

15 The Devil

The Devil signifies bondage and enslavement. It represents feeling trapped in a situation or chained by your addictions and choices. It can also imply that someone is being dishonest or manipulative.

OVERVIEW
The Devil generally signifies feeling trapped in a situation, which is often of your own choosing. Fear, attitudes and behaviour can keep you captive. The Devil suggests accepting responsibility for the situation.

LOVE
In a relationship, The Devil indicates that one or both partners feel trapped. Manipulation, jealousy and temptation can also be at play. If you are single, The Devil can indicate lust and unhealthy trysts.

CAREER
In a career context, The Devil has several meanings. This card can indicate that you feel trapped in your career and see no way out. It can also refer to deceit and hostility, so be careful who you trust.

SPIRITUALITY
In a spiritual reading, this card indicates that you have become too materialistic, and need to reconnect with nature.

ADVICE
Materialism and lust threaten to be your downfall. Face up to your addictions and find ways to overcome them. We can only break free of the cycle by fostering self-awareness and accepting our limitations.

DESCRIPTION
The Devil, part human, part animal, perches on a small black altar between a naked man and a woman. The couple resembles The Lovers card. His palm is tattooed with the symbol of Saturn (symbolising morality and rigidity). His left hand holds a torch. The couple are chained to a ring on the altar, but the chains are loosely fitted around their necks and could be slipped off, representing their choice to remain trapped. Their tails represent the Tree of Knowledge and the Tree of Life.

• DARKNESS • DANGER • OBSESSION • OPPRESSION • PERVERSITY • HOSTILITY • LUST

Celtic Cross Positions

1. **SIGNIFICATOR:** You are preoccupied with a controlling relationship or your inability to break free from a negative situation.

2. **OBSTACLES:** Represents temptation, sensation and physical pleasure. Feelings of entrapment, fear and danger.

3. **ROOT:** Self-oppression and poor decision-making. Reliance on physical pleasures and material possessions for happiness and fulfilment.

4. **PAST:** A recent negative situation. Perhaps you managed to break free, or perhaps you are still trapped.

5. **CROWN:** Temptation by physical or material pleasure. Becoming obsessed. You are heading in the wrong direction. A warning.

6. **NEAR FUTURE:** Represents entrapment. It suggests misuse of power, money or sex. You may be lured by temptation. It indicates something or someone to steer clear of. A warning.

7. **FEAR:** Physical or material over-indulgence or temptation. A fear of obsession, entrapment, oppression or use of force.

8. **JUDGEMENT:** Represents an individual who appears stuck in a negative situation or relationship. Someone who has sold out for money and favours. It may indicate a person who is sometimes cruel. It could also be someone who has made a terrible mistake.

9. **HOPE:** Represents hoping for physical and material pleasures. Virtue and goodness in exchange for immediate gratification.

10. **OUTCOME:** Represents weakness and the risk of succumbing to someone else's will or domination. It indicates not sticking up for your beliefs or being tempted by a cheap win. A warning to stick to your morals, especially in times of difficulty. A mistake now could be costly for all concerned. It may mean unscrupulous ambition. A warning.

OPPOSING CARDS

THE FOOL
having faith, believing

THE HIEROPHANT
faith, conformity, belief system

THE STAR
hope, faith, optimism

FOUR OF WANDS
freedom, release

SIX OF CUPS
goodwill, innocence, simple joys

TEN OF CUPS
joy, peace, blessings

REINFORCING CARDS

SEVEN OF CUPS
overindulgence, dissipation

EIGHT OF SWORDS
confusion, restriction

NINE OF SWORDS
despair, lack of joy

• RADICAL CHANGE • RELEASE • DOWNFALL • REVELATION • DISRUPTION • CATACLYSM

16 The Tower

DESCRIPTION
A tall grey tower is on fire after being struck by lightning. The Tower's golden crown (which symbolises pride and material status) is dislodged. Flames leap out from the tower's windows. Two figures are falling head-first. The background shows the black of night.

The Tower indicates a sudden, radical change. This will often be a life-changing event that is unexpected and chaotic. A major transformation is on your horizon.

OVERVIEW
The Tower represents trauma, chaos and destruction, the breaking of the old to make way for the new. Expect chaos and a time of excessive change, where the ground feels like it is shifting under your feet. This life-changing experience might seem petrifying, but it can be liberating. The Tower can also warn of tragic or traumatic events. Not an easy time, but unavoidable.

LOVE
The Tower can represent separation or divorce. It can also mean that one partner is going through a traumatic event. If you are single, you might meet someone who turns your world upside down.

CAREER
In a career reading, this card suggests a major change. You might lose your job or be made redundant. This will be a life-changing experience, but it is necessary for growth. It may lead you in directions previously unconsidered.

SPIRITUALITY
When this card appears in a spiritual reading, you can expect a major shift in your attitudes and beliefs. You may experience transformation and a sudden flash of truth.

ADVICE
There is no way to sugar-coat this card — dramatic changes are coming. Many of us fear change, and, as a result, would rather cling to what we know, even if it's not good for us. The Tower takes away this option. Change is coming whether you want it or not. So you might as well embrace it and enjoy the journey.

• CATASTROPHE • PURGING • TRAGEDY • SUDDEN ENLIGHTENMENT • CHAOS • DESTRUCTION

Celtic Cross Positions

1. **SIGNIFICATOR:** You are experiencing a catastrophic phase. Significant disruptions and a painful experience.

2. **OBSTACLES:** Represents complete upheaval. It indicates a catharsis, a blessing in disguise, a shock, revolutionary thoughts, ideas, and action.

3. **ROOT:** An unforeseen disruption will result in a catastrophe. Transformation and change. An unavoidable upset. A disaster waiting to happen.

4. **PAST:** Represents a severe catastrophe in your recent past. You lost something important or discovered a truth. A life-changing event.

5. **CROWN:** Represents the overthrow of an existing belief system, resulting in a sudden change in a circumstance, relationship, or situation. Looking for truth in a precarious situation.

6. **NEAR FUTURE:** A significant transformation is on the horizon. It will tear down the old to allow something new to be built. A complete overthrow of a situation or relationship.

7. **FEAR:** You fear that your efforts have been in vain and that your reasoning is wrong. It indicates a fear of disruption or truth.

8. **JUDGEMENT:** A person experiencing a tremendous upheaval. Someone looking for an escape from a bad situation. Or someone coming to terms with lies and dishonesty.

9. **HOPE:** You desire change or an escape from an oppressive situation. A desire to start over.

10. **OUTCOME:** Expect catastrophe, major upheaval, severe disruption and disaster. A cataclysmic shift. Something you once felt was important will be stripped from you. It will be painful, but it is a blessing in disguise. You are about to experience a major transformation as you enter the next stage of your life.

OPPOSING CARDS

THE CHARIOT
victory, control

TEMPERANCE
middle ground, contained, staying together

THE STAR
serenity, calmness

SIX OF WANDS
pride, acclaim

TEN OF CUPS
peace, serenity

REINFORCING CARDS

DEATH
sweeping impact, powerful forces

THE SUN
enlightenment, revelation

FIVE OF PENTACLES
hard times

• HOPE • INSPIRATION • GENEROSITY • SERENITY • SPIRITUAL LOVE • RADIANT ENERGY • RENEWAL

17 The Star

The Star symbolises hope and promise. If you have been going through a difficult time, The Star indicates that this is nearly over.

OVERVIEW
The Star is an uplifting and positive card. You might hear good news or realise a goal. You are likely feeling optimistic and believe in yourself at this moment. If you have an unrealised dream, The Star encourages you to follow it.

LOVE
The Star is a positive card for those in relationships, suggesting that all is going well. If you are single, this card indicates you might meet someone who will become special to you.

CAREER
You might be feeling inspired when this card appears in your reading. In a career context, good news and opportunities might be coming your way. If you have creative inspiration, The Star encourages you to follow it.

SPIRITUALITY
The Star encourages you to incorporate your spirituality into your daily life and find balance.

ADVICE
Embrace all the opportunities and goodwill being offered to you. Now is a very auspicious time in your life.

DESCRIPTION
A naked golden-haired woman kneels over a pool of water. She represents purity, truth, and the balance between the unconscious and the conscious. From one vase, she pours water into a pool, and from another onto the land. The five streams created symbolise the five senses. In the sky, a large eight-pointed star is surrounded by seven smaller ones. There are mountains in the distance, suggesting that troubles are far away.

• IDEALISM • OPTIMISM • INTUITION • A PROMISE • REJUVENATION

Celtic Cross Positions

1. **SIGNIFICATOR:** You are optimistic, intuitive and inspirational.

2. **OBSTACLES:** Indicates the necessity for healing and the power of renewal. It suggests peace and tranquillity.

3. **ROOT:** Represents illumination, inspiration and guidance from within. Acceptance, healing and peace.

4. **PAST:** Represents a recent period of peace and relaxation. You may have taken some time to recover from a difficult time or an illness.

5. **CROWN:** Represents a period of recovery, healing and peace. An opportunity to make a wish.

6. **NEAR FUTURE:** Represents the beginning of a self-care phase, filled with hope and inspiration. Healing from within. Wishes coming true. Recovery after a stressful period.

7. **FEAR:** A fear of losing hope or slowing down.

8. **JUDGEMENT:** Represents a radiant, idealistic and optimistic individual. Someone who possesses a unique inner beauty.

9. **HOPE:** You may be hoping for recovery or renewal of energy.

10. **OUTCOME:** Represents wishes or dreams come true. A time of peace and tranquillity. It may indicate healing. It offers bright prospects for the future. A good omen.

OPPOSING CARDS

THE DEVIL
hopelessness, lack of faith, pessimism

THE TOWER
upheaval, chaos

THE MOON
disturbed, troubled, anxious, bewildered

TWO OF SWORDS
blocked flow of feelings

NINE OF SWORDS
guilt, anguish, despair

REINFORCING CARDS

THE FOOL
innocence, faith, trust

THE EMPRESS
generosity, free flowing love

SIX OF CUPS
good will, sharing

TEN OF CUPS
joy, positive feeling, blessings

• IMAGINATION • INTUITION • FEAR • ILLUSION • BEWILDERMENT • THE UNKNOWN • UNCONSCIOUS

18 The Moon

When The Moon appears, things are not as they seem. It can indicate lies, deception and confusion. The Moon also tells you to listen to your intuition and pay attention to your dreams.

DESCRIPTION
A moon that is both waxing and waning hangs in the night sky. A dog and wolf howl at the moon, representing our fears. In the foreground is a pool of water. A path runs from the water's edge between the two animals, across the plains and between two single towers. A crayfish symbolises the need to let go of the past. The two grey towers in the turbulent ocean are reminiscent of The Tower card.

OVERVIEW
The Moon warns us that things are hidden from view or do not appear as they truly are. As such, it is difficult to know what to trust. It can indicate that an emotionally difficult time lies ahead or that you feel confused and unsure. The Moon advises you to trust only yourself during this time.

LOVE
In a relationship, The Moon indicates lies, deceit and high emotions. If you are single, The Moon suggests that someone is lying to you.

CAREER
The presence of The Moon in a career reading suggests that things are unclear. Be careful who you trust. Someone may be trying to manipulate or control things.

SPIRITUALITY
The Moon is a card of intuition and advises you to listen closely to your dreams and subconscious.

ADVICE
This is not an easy time. You might be imagining things that are not there because you are too focused on your feelings and emotions.

• LUNACY • HIDDEN DANGER • DREAMS • PSYCHIC POWERS • INTENSE FEELINGS • FANTASY

Celtic Cross Positions

1. **SIGNIFICATOR:** You are imaginative, intuitive, and guided by sympathy and compassion. You are experiencing the completion of one phase of personal growth.

2. **OBSTACLES:** Represents illusion, hidden danger, enemies and deception. It suggests the power and influence of unconscious thought.

3. **ROOT:** Murky subconscious influences, wild imagination and strong emotions. You are mixing fact with fiction, reality with dreams, the conscious with the unconscious.

4. **PAST:** Recovering deeply buried or unconscious memories from childhood. Possibly a period of dream therapy or journey writing. It may indicate deception or illusion.

5. **CROWN:** A time of confusion and doubt. You may have heightened awareness, creativity or intuition. Emotions are running high.

6. **NEAR FUTURE:** Represents an approach to the unknown, internal confusion or chaos. It indicates hidden danger or being an open target. Use caution.

7. **FEAR:** Represents a fear of the subconscious thoughts, intuition, imagination or dreams.

8. **JUDGEMENT:** Represents someone who is overly sensitive or emotionally unpredictable.

9. **HOPE:** Represents a desire for self-discovery through intuition, imagination, and dreams. You may be wishing for psychic ability and creativity.

10. **OUTCOME:** Represents the unknown. This is an essential time for dreams, intuition and ideas. A time of fluctuation and change. Strong emotions may make you feel depressed, irrational and confused. Hidden dangers may lie ahead. Not all is as it seems. Someone might be keeping a secret from you.

OPPOSING CARDS

THE STAR
serene, peaceful, untroubled

THE SUN
assurance, clarity, enlightenment

REINFORCING CARDS

SEVEN OF CUPS
illusions, fantasy, unrealistic ideals

TWO OF SWORDS
self-deception, not seeing the truth

EIGHT OF SWORDS
confusion, lack of clarity

• ENLIGHTENMENT • GREATNESS • ASSURANCE • REJUVENATION • CREATIVITY • JOY • ENERGY

19 The Sun

The Sun is a wonderful card to draw. It represents happiness, creativity and positive energy. This is a time to celebrate victories and jobs well done.

DESCRIPTION

A naked child holds a long red banner in his left hand (symbolising freedom from material constraints) while riding bareback on a grey horse. In the sky above is a huge golden-faced sun with rays that alternate between straight and undulating. In the background are the grey walls of a garden. Four sunflowers represent balance and stability, and the four elements of Air, Fire, Water, and Earth.

OVERVIEW
The Sun signifies that your troubles are over and good times lie ahead. Excellent news, the success of a project, and a new exciting relationship are all possibilities. It's a good luck card, so seize opportunities and enjoy the creative energy flowing into your life.

LOVE
The Sun is a positive relationship card, indicating a time of contentment and joy. If you are single, a new relationship might be on its way.

CAREER
In a career context, the Sun signifies success, such as a new job, a promotion or the successful launch of a project. It's a happy and fulfilling time, full of opportunities and energy.

SPIRITUALITY
Spiritually, the Sun is a card of positivity and enlightenment. This is a time to embrace, share and enjoy your spiritual path.

ADVICE
Happiness is coming your way. Don't feel guilty – you've earned this moment in the light.

• SPIRITUAL GROWTH • FULL LIFE • ABUNDANCE • VITALITY • CONTENTMENT • HAPPINESS

Celtic Cross Positions

1. **SIGNIFICATOR:** You are loving, warm and affectionate, full of life and vitality.

2. **OBSTACLES:** Represents fun, good health, love and happiness. Thoughts are directed towards personal growth.

3. **ROOT:** A favourable situation of activity, optimism and good health.

4. **PAST:** A recent time of accomplishments and happiness.

5. **CROWN:** Represents an upcoming period of joy, happiness and fun. An opportunity for pleasure and success.

6. **NEAR FUTURE:** Represents prosperity, successful business and career pursuits. It suggests strong and healthy relationships.

7. **FEAR:** You fear being over-exposed or having unbridled fun.

8. **JUDGEMENT:** A fun, exciting, optimistic and well-rounded individual. A good friend.

9. **HOPE:** You desire success, good health, and love. A desire for relationships to develop and grow.

10. **OUTCOME:** Represents success and a good outcome. It suggests good health, positive relationships, and a successful career. Everything is coming together, and your life is filled with happiness. This is a time to take it easy and have fun.

OPPOSING CARDS

THE MOON
confusion, illusion, fear, disorientation

EIGHT OF CUPS
weariness

FIVE OF PENTACLES
tired, feeling run down

SIX OF SWORDS
depressed, listless

TEN OF SWORDS
exhaustion, collapse

REINFORCING CARDS

THE TOWER
enlightenment, revelation

THE WORLD
accomplishment, great achievement

TWO OF WANDS
personal power, vitality, brilliance

SIX OF WANDS
acclaim, prominence

• JUDGEMENT • REBIRTH • INNER CALLING • ABSOLUTION • SPIRITUAL CHANGE • LIBERATION

20 Judgement

Judgement emphasises the importance of forgiveness and truth. It is a time of reckoning that will send your life in a new direction. You might have heard the call of destiny.

OVERVIEW
Judgement requires that you be held accountable for your actions before moving on to the next phase. It warns against jumping to conclusions before discovering all the facts. It is also a card of spiritual awakening, where you finally realise your destiny. Judgement tells us to take responsibility for our choices and not to blame others for circumstances in our lives.

LOVE
Judgement indicates that if your relationship is having difficulty, honesty and lack of judgement might bring things back into balance. If you are single, Judgement advises you not to jump into a new relationship.

CAREER
In a career reading, Judgement can indicate that you are being watched. You might have clarity on your future career and be able to take steps to achieve it.

SPIRITUALITY
Judgement suggests a spiritual awakening. Let the universe guide you.

ADVICE
Judgement calls you to action and requires you to stand up and be counted. You may feel unworthy, ashamed or unable to evaluate yourself truthfully.

DESCRIPTION
An angel blows a trumpet bearing the Greek cross (symbolising balanced forces). In the foreground are naked grey figures. The dead – a man, a child and a woman – acknowledge the angel by rising from their open graves. Their coffins float in the sea of the unconscious. In the background, another family is waking up from the dead. The trumpet heralds a call for action. The time is at hand. The wait is over.

• REWARD OR PUNISHMENT • KARMA • RENEWAL • EVALUATION • TRANSFORMATION

Celtic Cross Positions

1. **SIGNIFICATOR:** You have sound judgement and can go confidently from one life situation to another. A call to action.

2. **OBSTACLES:** An awakening, liberation or reckoning. A very crucial decision has been made.

3. **ROOT:** Represents starting over. A clean slate. The truth about a situation will become clear. You may hear your true calling.

4. **PAST:** Recent hard work or selfless actions were rewarded. Perhaps you were offered a chance to start again.

5. **CROWN:** You may come across an opportunity of a lifetime. This is the end of a period of dormancy and the beginning of action. You are filled with renewed energy.

6. **NEAR FUTURE:** Represents a calling, an opportunity to get something or do something. It suggests an awakening or rebirth. A time when the truth becomes clear.

7. **FEAR:** You are scared to put all your energy into something new in case you fail.

8. **JUDGEMENT:** Represents a person hoping for a new lifestyle, a new path to follow, a new meaning, or purpose in life.

9. **HOPE:** You desire to find your calling in life. Hoping to start over with a clean slate. A wish for spiritual cleansing.

10. **OUTCOME:** Starting over, rebirth, a change in consciousness, liberation, and release from a period of inactivity. It suggests a settlement, decision or final determination. A good card for those who have acted with honour and integrity.

OPPOSING CARDS

DEATH
death, endings, departure

FIVE OF CUPS
regret, mistakes

NINE OF SWORDS
guilt, blame, despair

REINFORCING CARDS

THE FOOL
rebirth, new beginnings, new start

JUSTICE
deciding, accepting responsibility for errors

SEVEN OF PENTACLES
decisions already made

• COMPLETION • INVOLVEMENT • FULFILMENT • INTEGRATION • COMPLETE CYCLE

21 The World

The World symbolises the completion of the cycle. You've achieved what you set out to do and can feel proud of yourself. It can also suggest travel. The World is a very positive card.

DESCRIPTION

A woman with a purple scarf draped over her holds a double-terminated wand in each hand (symbolic of the ongoing renewal of life). She dances in the sky, encircled by a laurel ring (symbolising success and triumph). The red scarves above and below resemble a cross and symbolises balance. In each corner are creatures (an angel, an eagle, a lion and a bull) representing the four elements (Air, Water, Fire and Earth) and corresponding to Scorpio, Aquarius, Leo and Taurus.

OVERVIEW
The World is a card of completion and achievement. You have worked hard to get here and are about to take a well-deserved break. You may feel on top of the world. It implies that you have been successful (in your work, or relationship, or general life situation). Grab new opportunities with both hands. Travel might be in your future.

LOVE
In a romance reading, The World represents a loving and committed relationship. If you are single, this card suggests you will meet someone special soon.

CAREER
In a career context, The World suggests that you have achieved your goal and are experiencing success. A new opportunity may be on the horizon. You may travel for work. An auspicious time of good energy and excitement.

SPIRITUALITY
In a spiritual context, The World signifies fulfilment and suggests that you have learnt important lessons.

ADVICE
You might be living your life according to other peoples' expectations. Perhaps it is time to discover what you really want out of life.

• TRIUMPH • ACCOMPLISHMENT • SUCCESS • THINGS COME TOGETHER

Celtic Cross Positions

1. **SIGNIFICATOR:** You are happy with yourself and the world. Your sense of fulfilment comes from your positive state of mind.

2. **OBSTACLES:** Completion, wholeness and the freedom that comes with having a specific goal in mind.

3. **ROOT:** Indicates feeling on top of the world. Success, fulfilment and happiness in all facets of life.

4. **PAST:** Completion of an important stage or reaching a goal. A time of great opportunities and options. Many things have come together, giving you the freedom to move forward.

5. **CROWN:** Represents completion of something or a life lesson. You are on top of the world. You have all the tools for achieving fulfilment and success.

6. **NEAR FUTURE:** Represents a sense of completion, wholeness and attainment. A time for ultimate freedom. Achieving an important goal.

7. **FEAR:** You fear failure, losing everything and not achieving your destiny.

8. **JUDGEMENT:** Represents an individual who is prosperous and free to move in any direction.

9. **HOPE:** You desire to complete this life stage or current goal. You may desire liberation and freedom.

10. **OUTCOME:** Represents completion and indicates a sense of triumph on reaching an important goal. It suggests spiritual attainment and indicates a reward for completion. You are free to move, act or decide what path you will follow.

OPPOSING CARDS

THE HERMIT
isolation, disengaging

FOUR OF CUPS
lack of involvement, withdrawal

FIVE OF WANDS
lack of integration, at cross purposes

REINFORCING CARDS

TEMPERANCE
integration, combination, synthesis

THE SUN
accomplishment, achievements

NINE OF CUPS
achieving your heart's desire

TEN OF CUPS
happiness, emotional fulfilment

TEN OF PENTACLES
affluence, material fulfilment

The Minor Arcana

The Minor Arcana is divided into 4 suits, each containing 14 cards. While the Major Arcana expresses major life lessons, the Minor Arcana cards represent the concerns, activities and emotions that make up our everyday lives. Each suit has a unique quality.

CUPS - PAGE 55
Cups is the suit of emotions and is associated with the element of water. It describes our inner states, feelings and relationship patterns.

PENTACLES - PAGE 85
Pentacles is the suit of material concerns and is associated with the element of earth. It represents prosperity, wealth, practicality and security.

SWORDS - PAGE 115
Swords is the suit of intellect and is associated with the element of air. It is concerned with justice, truth, thought and logic.

WANDS - PAGE 145
Wands is the suit of creativity and is associated with the element of fire. It is concerned with action, movement, enthusiasm, adventure and confidence.

The Structure of the Suits

Each suit contains 10 numbered cards (Ace to 10) and 4 court cards (Page, Knight, Queen and King).

ACES
Each Ace represents the qualities of its suit and indicates new beginnings. They have a positive influence.

NUMBERED CARDS 2 - 10
Each numbered card expresses different situations and emotions which are connected to the quality of the suit.

COURT CARDS
The court cards usually represent a person. The Page is a younger person or someone young at heart. The Knight is a young adult. The Queen is a mature female or feminine influence and the King represents a mature male or masculine influence. These cards can also represent a situation.

The Suit of Cups

The Suit of Cups rules the emotions and symbolises love, family and happiness. It is associated with creativity, relationships and imagination.

If there are many Cups in a reading, you are likely thinking with your heart and not your head.

The negative side of Cups includes being overly emotional or emotionally withdrawn, unable to express yourself or lacking creativity.

Element: Water

Keywords: friendship, compassion, creativity, emotion, sensitivity, love

Corresponding playing card suit: Hearts

Astrological signs: Pisces, Cancer and Scorpio

Noted for: moods and emotions

Ace of Cups

new beginnings

Two of Cups

emotional bonds, love

Three of Cups

celebration, friendships

Four of Cups

depression, self-doubt

Five of Cups

sadness, misfortune

Six of Cups

nostalgia, innocence

Seven of Cups

opportunities, self-indulgence

Eight of Cups

ending, sacrifice

Nine of Cups

prosperity, wishes fulfilled

Ten of Cups

family, happiness

Page of Cups

news, intuition

Knight of Cups

new opportunities

Queen of Cups

compassion, calmness

King of Cups

idealistic, caring

• NEW BEGINNINGS • A NEW RELATIONSHIP • HAPPINESS • CELEBRATION

Ace of Cups

The Ace of Cups symbolises good fortune, new relationships and creative energy. A promise of abundance and exciting possibilities. It represents a gift or opportunity.

OVERVIEW
The Ace of Cups signifies new beginnings, usually in love and creativity. If you've been in a creative slump, this card hints that you'll soon be bursting with ideas. Good news, celebrations and romance are all possibilities.

LOVE
If you're single, the Ace of Cups suggests that a deep, fulfilling love will soon come into your life. For those in a relationship, your bond will likely strengthen. A wedding, engagement or pregnancy might be on the horizon.

CAREER
If you're looking for a change in career or feel that you've been stagnating, this card is a good omen. Its creative energy promises movement and inspiration. New possibilities, ideas and creative energy. It can suggest the beginning of an exciting venture.

SPIRITUALITY
A sign of a deeper connection to spirituality, follow the omens and trust your intuition. You may find yourself overflowing with spiritual connection. A time to get involved in more spiritual aspects of relationships.

ADVICE
Although a positive card, it does not encourage being passive. You need to actively help matters along. It also warns of the danger of unhealthy infatuation and obsession.

DESCRIPTION
A hand in the clouds holds an overflowing cup above an ocean filled with lotus blossoms. The dove symbolises love and fidelity. The letter on the cup is the Hebrew letter 'Mem', representing water. The cup symbolising intuition and emotions, overflowing with blessings. The five streams flowing from the cup represent the five senses. Five is also the sign of marriage. The lotus is a universal symbol of creation, fertility and human potential. Finally, water is associated with fertility and emotions.

• INTIMACY • PREGNANCY • ABUNDANCE • SPIRITUAL AWAKENING

Celtic Cross Positions

1. **SIGNIFICATOR:** You are a creative individual with a great capacity to love. You are tantalised by life and its possibilities.

2. **OBSTACLES:** Represents new beginnings, especially in love and relationships. It can indicate someone who is letting emotions take over from reality.

3. **ROOT:** A desire for a relationship or a new beginning. A desire to connect spiritually. Wishing for a relationship controls your thoughts and decision-making process.

4. **PAST:** Represents a deep past love. This relationship, or the feelings it evoked, is affecting you at the moment. It could also refer to a time of contentment and happiness, or a period of exceptional creativity.

5. **CROWN:** You are experiencing the happy feelings of a new relationship or a pleasant phase in an existing partnership.

6. **NEAR FUTURE:** A new love affair or burst of creativity is on the horizon. A positive beginning. A new perspective. Marriage, pregnancy, happiness and good fortune.

7. **FEAR:** You fear not being worthy, either romantically or creatively. Perhaps you fear commitment, letting go and trusting your heart.

8. **JUDGEMENT:** Represents a person with a profound capacity to give and receive love.

9. **HOPE:** You desire a meaningful relationship that offers a deep spiritual connection. A wish for more meaning in life.

10. **OUTCOME:** Represents good fortune and wishes coming true. An emotional or spiritual awakening. An auspicious relationship, love blossoming. It can also symbolise good news, new friendships, birth or a deepening spiritual connection.

OPPOSING CARDS

TEN OF WANDS
struggle, difficulty

TEN OF SWORDS
failure, endings

REINFORCING CARDS

THE EMPRESS
fertility, birth

THE LOVERS
love, marriage

ACE-ACE PAIRS

An Ace-Ace pair indicates that a new spirit is entering your life, drawing on the energy of the Ace of Cups (deep feelings, intimacy, compassion, love), plus one of these:

ACE OF PENTACLES
prosperity, abundance, trust, security

ACE OF SWORDS
intelligence, reason, justice, truth, clarity

ACE OF WANDS
creativity, excitement, adventure, courage

1 Beginning

• NEW PHASE • RECONCILIATION • LOVE • KINDRED SOULS • PARTNERSHIP • CONNECTION

Two of Cups

The Two of Cups symbolises the coming together of two people. A new phase of love or partnership. It is also the traditional card of contracts and agreements.

OVERVIEW
This card suggests a new mutually beneficial relationship, whether love, friendship or professional. It brings a sense of cooperation, harmony and balance. Two souls united in a common purpose.

LOVE
The Two of Cups promises magnetic attraction and a loving union. If you are in a relationship, this card suggests that your love will enter a new phase. If you've been having difficulties, this card indicates that they'll be overcome and passion will be reignited. If you are single and have met someone, the Two of Cups hints that it could become a meaningful relationship. Marriage proposals are also possible.

CAREER
A mutually beneficial partnership is on the horizon. The Two of Cups also suggests a contract will soon be signed. It encourages you to form relationships in the workplace.

SPIRITUALITY
In a spiritual reading, this card indicates meeting someone strongly connected to the spirit. Deep discussions and sharing spiritual beliefs. It is a time for working magically with others and finding balance and harmony.

ADVICE
This card encourages you to be optimistic and have faith.

DESCRIPTION
A young man and woman, exchange cups and pledge their love for one another. His outfit is similar to The Fool, while hers has a resemblance to The High Priestess. Above them floats the Caduceus of Hermes – a winged staff with two snakes wrapped around it, which is the ancient symbol of commerce, trade, and exchange. At the top of the caduceus is a lion's head, signifying passion and energy which suggests that there may be a lot of fiery, sexual energy between these two people.

• ATTRACTION • HARMONY • DEEP BOND • CONTRACTS • AGREEMENTS

Celtic Cross Positions

1. **SIGNIFICATOR:** You crave a deep romantic bond. You might be preoccupied with thoughts of your partner.

2. **OBSTACLES:** Love governs your decision-making process and thoughts.

3. **ROOT:** A new, meaningful relationship (either professional or emotional) is at the heart of the situation. It could indicate an existing relationship or your desire for one. A wish for harmony, understanding and communication.

4. **PAST:** A relationship or partnership has ended but weighs heavily on the mind and still influences your decisions.

5. **CROWN:** A new relationship or partnership may be coming into your life. A choice might need to be made.

6. **NEAR FUTURE:** A new partnership or romance may lie in your future. A possible test of love or being required to make a commitment.

7. **FEAR:** You are worried about trusting others or being responsible for them, whether in a romantic relationship or business partnership.

8. **JUDGEMENT:** Represents an easily swayed individual, someone obsessed with being in a relationship.

9. **HOPE:** You hope for love and commitment.

10. **OUTCOME:** A relationship with physical and spiritual benefits. A choice in love and commitment or marriage. It is a situation of give and take, a sense of cooperation. Entering a new phase. Finalising a contract or business partnership.

OPPOSING CARDS

THE HERMIT
needing to be alone, solitude

FIVE OF WANDS
disagreement, staying apart, no peace

FOUR OF CUPS
self-absorbed, being alone

FIVE OF CUPS
broken relationship

REINFORCING CARDS

THE LOVERS
union, marriage, connection

TEMPERANCE
connection, working together

TEN OF CUPS
family relationships, bonding

TWO OF PENTACLES
balancing, finding the right mix

2 Duality, balance, harmony, reflection

• CELEBRATION • JOY • ABUNDANCE • GOOD NEWS • FRIENDSHIP

Three of Cups

DESCRIPTION

Three women dance in a circle, holding up their cups in a toast. There is a sense of kindred spirits. On the ground lies the harvest, symbolising abundance. It also reminds us that you reap what you sow. The card highlights the feminine aspect which draws together and unifies.

Celebration and friendship are the basis of this card. Sharing happiness, being kind, and lifting others up. Can signify the end of a difficult or lonely time.

OVERVIEW
The Three of Cups represents celebration and friendships. Good news, energy and receiving assistance or gifts. A time to make plans, spread out and interact with new people. If you've been in solitude for a while, now is the time to rejoin the dance of life and connect with others.

LOVE
If you are in a relationship, this card implies that things are going well. A celebration might be coming, such as a house-warming, wedding, engagement or baby shower. If you are single, there is a possibility that you will connect with someone soon.

CAREER
A work celebration, perhaps a launch or promotion, might be coming your way. It can also indicate a job offer to join a new team. If you work alone, perhaps it is time to involve others in your creative ideas.

SPIRITUALITY
A time of personal growth. Your next spiritual phase might be linked to joining others or becoming part of a group. Find a way to share abundance and harmony.

ADVICE
Spread out and interact with new people, but be selective about who you confide in. If you've recently had a stressful time, take some time out to recuperate.

• EXCITEMENT • COMMUNITY • KINDNESS • KINSHIP

Celtic Cross Positions

1 SIGNIFICATOR: You are a generous and optimistic person. Someone who values friendship and puts others' needs before your own.

2 OBSTACLES: You are so preoccupied with the destination that you may have forgotten to enjoy the journey.

3 ROOT: You seek the approval of others and crave friendship and a sense of belonging.

4 PAST: A past success and celebration. You might have met someone special.

5 CROWN: You have reached the successful completion of a project. You deserve time off to celebrate. Happiness, success, community, gratitude.

6 NEAR FUTURE: A celebration. The completion of a project. Marriage, birth, fertility. Valuable friendships.

7 FEAR: You are afraid of trusting others or worried about letting them down. You may fear loneliness.

8 JUDGEMENT: Represents an artistic and creative individual who seems to have everything they need and is socially accepted.

9 HOPE: You hope for a successful outcome of a project. A desire to have children or get married.

10 OUTCOME: Represents a celebration, the coming together of several elements. An unexpected reunion. A happy outcome. Hopes and dreams achieved.

OPPOSING CARDS

THE HERMIT
being solitary, withdrawing from group

NINE OF WANDS
lack of trust, wariness

THREE OF SWORDS
lonely, isolated, hurting

SIX OF SWORDS
sad, depressed

NINE OF SWORDS
anguished, joyless

REINFORCING CARDS

THE HIEROPHANT
focusing on the group

TEMPERANCE
joining forces, working together

FOUR OF WANDS
excitement, high spirits, celebration

THREE OF PENTACLES
working in a group

3 Trio, planning, ideas, creation

• UNMOTIVATED • DISCONTENTMENT • BOREDOM • APATHY • SELF-DOUBT

Four of Cups

The Four of Cups expresses regret, sadness and depression. A time when life seems boring. Retreating from the world and focusing on the negative. This card suggests self-absorption, depression and laziness.

OVERVIEW
The Four of Cups signifies a time of feeling emotionally stuck and stagnant. Perhaps you regret things you've done or opportunities that you've missed. It may feel as though the colour has faded from the world. It might also signify the natural calm after a busy time. Opportunities are available, but you can't see them.

LOVE
If you are in a relationship, this card can indicate that you are feeling bored with it. Perhaps one or both of you have become complacent. It might also be a natural pause. It hints at regret over past mistakes.

CAREER
The Four of Cups can indicate that you feel bored or unfulfilled in your work. No enthusiasm to complete projects. A time of rest and recuperation after a stressful time.

SPIRITUALITY
If you are feeling spiritually stagnant, a spiritual retreat may refresh you. Take stock, count your blessings.

ADVICE
Don't remain stuck in listlessness. While taking time out is fine, make sure that you don't wallow in self pity. Forgive yourself for past mistakes and move on.

DESCRIPTION
This card shows a young man sitting under a tree with his arms crossed, deep in contemplation or meditation. He is so engrossed in his thoughts that he does not notice the outstretched arm offering a cup. A further three cups stand at his feet, but he doesn't seem to notice or care about these new opportunities either.

• STAGNATION • DEPRESSION • WITHDRAWAL • REGRET • STUCK IN A RUT

Celtic Cross Positions

1. **SIGNIFICATOR:** You are going through a period of depression, which has led to withdrawal from those around you.

2. **OBSTACLES:** You are wallowing in self-pity, which stops you from seeing the opportunities that are available.

3. **ROOT:** Regret over past actions has led to this situation and prevents you from seeing the positives in life.

4. **PAST:** Represents a period of stagnation. Regret over past mistakes. Feeling disillusioned by your own actions. A period of depression.

5. **CROWN:** An opportunity for growth and self-awareness. Breaking free from negative thoughts. Reaching out to others. Reconnecting with the world.

6. **NEAR FUTURE:** A time of contemplation. A time to withdraw and be passive. Don't allow depression to take you. Rather, focus on what you can be grateful for.

7. **FEAR:** You fear being stuck in a rut, of being alone or depressed.

8. **JUDGEMENT:** Represents a loner who doesn't reach out to others. Someone wrapped up in their own issues.

9. **HOPE:** You wish to connect with others and break free from the cycle of apathy and depression. To rise above the feeling of apathy and embrace life again.

10. **OUTCOME:** Represents a time of solitude. Time spent alone to work through the emotions you feel. Time to forgive yourself and others. Healing and recuperation after a period of stress.

OPPOSING CARDS

THE WORLD
involvement, caring, taking part

FOUR OF WANDS
excitement, optimism high energy,

TWO OF CUPS
connection, sharing with others

EIGHT OF PENTACLES
making an effort, working hard

REINFORCING CARDS

THE HERMIT
withdrawing, being introverted

FOUR OF SWORDS
contemplating, taking time alone

SIX OF SWORDS
listless, depressed

4 Stability, order, making things happen

• SADNESS • LOSS • GRIEVING • DISAPPOINTMENT • LEGACIES

Five of Cups

The Five of Cups symbolises grief and despair. Something important has been lost — a friendship, lover or relative. This card also signifies inheritance, a gift from someone who has passed.

DESCRIPTION
Three cups have been knocked over, their contents spilling onto the sand. A man stares at them – they symbolise his disappointments and failures. Behind him are two upright cups, which represent new opportunities. But the man is so focused on his loss that he doesn't notice these two cups. In the background, a bridge crosses a river. On the other side is a home, offering security. To reach it, the man must overcome his loss and move forward.

OVERVIEW
This card speaks of loss in all its forms. A heartbreak caused by a divorce or separation or bereavement caused by the death of a loved one. It can also indicate feelings of loneliness or abandonment. This card also reminds us to look for the positive. If you've lost a lover, you've perhaps gained experience and lessons. If a relative has passed away, perhaps a gift or inheritance is coming.

LOVE
You might be coming to terms with a recent break-up or are in a relationship that is not going well. This card symbolises divorce and separation. You may be feeling regret or guilt.

CAREER
This card can indicate business failure or job loss. It can also suggest that a business partner might abandon the business. Not all is lost, so look for the positives.

SPIRITUALITY
In a spiritual reading, this card can indicate that you are stagnating and failing to see the positives in life. Spending time in nature might help you to reconnect.

ADVICE
Shift your focus to the present and leave thoughts of the past behind. Although you have lost something or someone, you have also gained something. Embrace the change. It is time to let go and move forward.

• INHERITANCE • SILVER LINING • REGRET • MISFORTUNE • REMORSE

Celtic Cross Positions

1. **SIGNIFICATOR:** You are focusing on the negative and ignoring the positive aspects of the situation.

2. **OBSTACLES:** You may feel like a victim and blame others for the situation, but you need to accept the role you played.

3. **ROOT:** An ending or loss of a relationship, idea or dream. Possibly a death.

4. **PAST:** A previous loss or mistake is linked to the issue at hand and weighs heavily on your mind. You cannot move on until you accept and forgive, or come to terms with your loss.

5. **CROWN:** The end of something is approaching. Sadness and grief cast a shadow over you.

6. **NEAR FUTURE:** Something important has been lost which has filled you with sadness. A time of grief, sorrow and regret.

7. **FEAR:** You fear change, loss or ending up all alone. Also a fear of making a mistake and having to live with the consequences.

8. **JUDGEMENT:** Represents someone who has given up hope. Someone who is grieving and unable to connect with others.

9. **HOPE:** Represents a desire for the current situation to end. Hoping to leave the past behind.

10. **OUTCOME:** Represents a lost relationship, situation, or event. Something is coming to an end. Drastic change. But not all is lost, as endings are also beginnings. Two cups remain full — focus on what you have, not what you've lost.

OPPOSING CARDS

THE LOVERS
establishing a relationship

JUDGEMENT
absolving yourself, releasing regret

SIX OF WANDS
triumph, winning

TWO OF CUPS
relationship

NINE OF CUPS
contentment, satisfaction

REINFORCING CARDS

DEATH
loss, good-byes

THREE OF SWORDS
separation, loss of love, heartache

SIX OF SWORDS
sadness

FIVE OF PENTACLES
rejection, lack of support or approval

5 Adaptation, challenge, conflict

• CHILDHOOD • NOSTALGIA • REUNION • INNOCENCE

Six of Cups

The Six of Cups symbolises childhood and innocence. It is a card of simple happiness, kindness and nostalgia. Memories of old plans, past friendships and dreams resurface.

OVERVIEW
This card suggests that you are feeling nostalgic or have recently met someone from your past. Can also indicate that you are spending too much time thinking about times gone by. If you have had a difficult time recently, this card may be telling you to accept the support of family and friends.

LOVE
If you are single, perhaps a past lover will be coming back into your life. If you are in a relationship, this card hints at shared warm, simple and rejuvenating love. It can also suggest problems that are caused by acting immaturely or childishly.

CAREER
In a career reading, this card is a good omen. It indicates creativity, sharing and kindness. It also hints that brushing up on old skills would be a good use of your time.

SPIRITUALITY
This card encourages exchanging gifts and sharing information. This can be carried across into your spiritual practices. Try to keep things simple and wholesome.

ADVICE
Are you romanticising a past event or relationship? If thoughts of the past are consuming you, allow the old memories to inspire and encourage you – perhaps you need to pursue an old dream or hobby? A warning against the tendency to not take responsibility for your actions.

DESCRIPTION
A boy gives a cup to a girl. All cups on the card are filled with flowers, symbolising beauty, youth and springtime. The children represent childhood memories. In the background, an adult walks away, showing the space between the present and the past. The house behind them symbolises safety and comfort.

• SIMPLICITY • PLAYFULNESS • MEMORIES • INNER CHILD

Celtic Cross Positions

1. **SIGNIFICATOR:** You are innocent at heart and find joy in almost every situation.

2. **OBSTACLES:** Represents the importance of the past and our roots. The value of listening to the child within and embracing simple pleasures.

3. **ROOT:** Family or past relationships lie at the heart of this issue. Perhaps connecting with someone from your past has made this reading necessary.

4. **PAST:** Represents a time that you look back on with fond memories. It can also suggest a past relationship that still affects you.

5. **CROWN:** A longing to be with family. Nostalgia for times past. Renewal of old hobbies and friendships. A warning not to dwell on the past too much.

6. **NEAR FUTURE:** A time of simplicity, openness and naïvety. A meeting of old friends, a visit to a childhood memory. A reunion.

7. **FEAR:** You fear memories of the past.

8. **JUDGEMENT:** A happy individual with childlike innocence and excitement. Someone filled with hope.

9. **HOPE:** You wish for things to return to how they were before. You might also want children.

10. **OUTCOME:** This represents a time of new ideas and rejuvenation. Imagination bursting with inspiration and creativity. Lessons from the past should be remembered as the future is planned.

OPPOSING CARDS

THE DEVIL
negativity, corruption, coveting

THE MOON
false memory, misplaced nostalgia

NINE OF WANDS
lack of innocence, believing the worst

FIVE OF SWORDS
cynical, hostile, selfish

SEVEN OF SWORDS
deceiving, manipulating

NINE OF SWORDS
guilty

REINFORCING CARDS

THE STAR
sharing, old relationship might be rekindled

THE SUN
old relationship might be rekindled

TEN OF CUPS
feeling blessed, happy, joyful

6 Patterns, togetherness

• TOO MUCH CHOICE • SELF-INDULGENCE • OPTIONS • OPPORTUNITIES

Seven of Cups

The Seven of Cups symbolises having too much choice and the negative aspects of this. It can also suggest wishful thinking and being unrealistic about what can be achieved. This card serves as a reminder that things are not always as they seem.

OVERVIEW
The Seven of Cups represents having many options to choose from, which may cause you to feel overwhelmed and unable to make a decision. The Seven of Cups also signifies that you are indulging in daydreaming instead of taking proactive steps to improve your situation.

LOVE
If you are single, this card indicates many romance opportunities may make themselves available to you. A choice might be difficult to make. If you are in a relationship, the Seven of Cups can suggest that a new love interest may enter your life and cause you to question your existing relationship. It can also signify that you are fantasising too much about your partner.

CAREER
In a career context, this card suggests you'll face some tough choices soon. You cannot pursue all opportunities offered, so you will need to consider the options carefully. It can also be a reminder that hard work is necessary to make dreams come true.

SPIRITUALITY
In a spiritual context, this card indicates that you may be interested in many different forms of spiritual practice.

ADVICE
Nothing will come from nothing, you need to put in the work.
Your fantasies might be preventing you from moving on. This card can also be a warning to be careful about what you decide.

DESCRIPTION
A man stands before seven cups filled with various gifts. Some cups contain desirable gifts such as jewels, but others hold curses, such as the snake or dragon. The clouds and the cups symbolise the man's wishes and dreams, and the different offerings suggest that you need to be careful what you wish for, as not everything is as it seems. Choices must be made, but in doing so, you must go beyond illusion and allure and instead focus on what's right for you.

• DECISIONS • PROCRASTINATION • ILLUSION • WISHFUL THINKING

Celtic Cross Positions

1. **SIGNIFICATOR:** You are constantly filled with possibilities. You are easily distracted by new ideas, which prevents you from making progress.

2. **OBSTACLES:** You dream about what you want instead of working practically towards a goal.

3. **ROOT:** Suggests that you are trapped in limbo because you are unsure of what you want.

4. **PAST:** A choice made in the past affects the current situation. Perhaps the wrong choice has caused regret. It might also represent a time of indecisiveness, when making a decision seemed impossible.

5. **CROWN:** The options on offer are numerous and can lead to feeling overwhelmed. More information is needed before a decision can be made.

6. **NEAR FUTURE:** Represents an upcoming choice. An important decision will need to be made soon. Make sure that you have all the necessary information in order to make an informed decision.

7. **FEAR:** You fear indecisiveness and procrastination.

8. **JUDGEMENT:** An individual who is seeking advice. Or someone who is self-indulgent and spoilt for choice.

9. **HOPE:** You desire many things. You are easily distracted and unable to focus on one thing.

10. **OUTCOME:** An important choice will need to be made. The time for procrastination and dreaming is over. Now is the time to make decisions and take charge of your destiny.

OPPOSING CARDS

THE MAGICIAN
focus, commitment

THE EMPEROR
discipline, structure

TEMPERANCE
balance, moderation

FOUR OF PENTACLES
order, control

EIGHT OF PENTACLES
working hard, applying yourself

NINE OF PENTACLES
discipline, restraint, refinement

REINFORCING CARDS

THE DEVIL
overindulgence, dissipation

THE MOON
illusions, fantasy, unrealistic ideas

NINE OF CUPS
sensual excess

7 Accomplishments, self-expansion

• CHANGING DIRECTION • TRANSITION • SACRIFICE • ENDING • MOVING AWAY • CLARITY

Eight of Cups

The Eight of Cups symbolises choosing to walk away from something, such as a relationship, career or creative project. A time of transition during which a cycle ends and a new one begins. A feeling of sadness and disillusionment as you go in search of a deeper meaning to life.

OVERVIEW
The Eight of Cups represents abandoning plans or relationships and choosing a different path. Everything has a beginning and an end, and this card shows that you've recognised that change needs to happen in order to grow. It takes great courage to walk away, and it can also come with feelings of guilt and anxiety.

LOVE
If you are in a relationship, the Eight of Cups can signify either you or your partner walking away. Even if the separation seems inevitable, the decision can still be difficult. If you are single, the Eight of Cups can indicate feeling lonely or being wary of starting a new relationship.

CAREER
This card can indicate the ending of a business or career path. It may also signify the necessity of walking away from an unsuccessful project or business concept. You may need to explore different ideas or approach the situation from a different angle.

SPIRITUALITY
The Eight of Cups indicates that you may be heading into a period of self-discovery. By going in a different direction, you might discover your purpose.

ADVICE
As the saying goes, change is the only constant in life. It's time to head in a new direction, and instead of feeling depressed, try to look for the positive elements this will bring to your future.

DESCRIPTION
Eight unbalanced cups stand in the foreground. A figure walks away from them into the unknown. It feels as though a cup is missing – a sign that emotional fulfilment is lacking. The character has turned away from cups to shuffle away into the mountains. The river symbolises emotions, and the mountains represent the awareness that this journey will not be easy. The moon shows two faces – new and full – implying that one cycle must end before the other can begin.

• SOBRIETY • FEELING TRAPPED • AVOIDING ISSUES • DECISIVENESS • DISILLUSIONMENT

Celtic Cross Positions

1. **SIGNIFICATOR:** You are currently disillusioned with life as you've realised that a sacrifice needs to be made.

2. **OBSTACLES:** It might be time to physically withdraw from the situation while you think about the best course of action. You may need to leave things you care about behind in order to chase your dreams.

3. **ROOT:** Knowing that it is time to move on weighs heavily on your mind. Although the decision is inevitable, it is still difficult to walk away.

4. **PAST:** Represents having left behind a situation, relationship or career. The effects of this decision are still being felt.

5. **CROWN:** You are moving towards better things, leaving behind bad choices or something that has reached the end of its cycle. Sadness hangs over the situation, but this will pass.

6. **NEAR FUTURE:** A time of transition. Walking away from something that no longer has value in the future. You need to change direction in order to follow your destiny.

7. **FEAR:** You fear feeling trapped or ending up alone.

8. **JUDGEMENT:** Represents someone who runs when things get complicated. Someone who has often been disappointed in love.

9. **HOPE:** You hope for a better future and that you have made the right decision by walking away.

10. **OUTCOME:** You have decided to walk away from a situation. Cutting your losses, making a sacrifice or taking a journey. The road ahead may not be easy, but pain is sometimes necessary for growth and achieving your dreams.

OPPOSING CARDS

STRENGTH
endurance, strength

THE SUN
vitality, high energy

NINE OF WANDS
hanging on, persevering

REINFORCING CARDS

THE HERMIT
searching for deeper meaning

DEATH
moving on, leaving

THREE OF WANDS
going on a trip, going into new territory

EIGHT OF WANDS
finishing up, ending a chapter

SIX OF SWORDS
moving on, going on a trip

8 Inspiration, structure, balance

• SATISFACTION • ZEST FOR LIFE • WISHES COMING TRUE • REALISING DREAMS • HAPPINESS

Nine of Cups

The Nine of Cups is the traditional wish card of the Tarot. It is said that when you draw this card, you have the genie and will receive whatever you wish. Success is on the way.

OVERVIEW
The Nine of Cups indicates your wishes coming true or the realisation of a dream. It promises prosperity and recognition. It also means having self-confidence but warns against becoming over-indulgent. It is a card of celebrations and a time of incredible happiness. Enjoying sensual pleasures and luxury. Being content with the world.

LOVE
If you are in a relationship, it is likely to be emotionally fulfilling and satisfying. If you are single, the Nine of Cups indicates that you are in a very healthy mental and emotional place. You have learned from past experiences, and this will be of great value in future relationships.

CAREER
This card tells you that success is on its way and that you should feel proud of your achievements. If you have a project in the wings or a business idea, now is the time to put your time and energy into it. It is likely to bring you success.

SPIRITUALITY
Indicates that you are feeling spiritually fulfilled and radiating positive energy.

ADVICE
Take pride in your achievements, but don't become complacent or smug. This card also warns against over-indulgence. While you have the wish card, it's important to know what you really want.

DESCRIPTION
A man sits alone on a wooden bench with crossed arms. His smile glows with satisfaction. Behind him is a curved shelf covered in a blue cloth. On this, nine cups have been placed. The cups represent fulfilled wishes and goals.

• PROSPERITY • ACHIEVEMENTS • REWARDS • CONFIDENCE • HIGH SELF-ESTEEM • TRIUMPH

Celtic Cross Positions

1 SIGNIFICATOR: You feel satisfied with yourself. You have achieved a great deal and have reason to feel proud.

2 OBSTACLES: Being full of yourself stops you from seeing others' points of view. Smugness evokes feelings of envy.

3 ROOT: Feeling that you are on top of the world. Success, fulfilment, happiness. Confidence and a will to succeed.

4 PAST: Represents the completion of a project. A time of great opportunities. Many things coming together.

5 CROWN: Completion of something important. You have a reason to be proud. Avoid over-indulgence and complacency. Constant work is required to stay on top.

6 NEAR FUTURE: An auspicious time lies ahead. Projects will be successfully completed, and dreams may come true.

7 FEAR: You are scared of losing what you have acquired.

8 JUDGEMENT: You are considered to be confident and successful. Some may be jealous of your achievements.

9 HOPE: A desire to be successful and realise your dreams. A wish for creative fulfilment and financial security.

10 OUTCOME: Completion and a sense of triumph. Rewards and wishes coming true. Luck is tilted in your favour. Now is the time to be bold. Represents success and the realisation of a dream.

OPPOSING CARDS

THE HERMIT
focusing less on the senses

FIVE OF CUPS
regret

REINFORCING CARDS

THE EMPRESS
enjoying the senses

THE LOVERS
sexual pleasure

THE WORLD
achieving your heart's desire

SIX OF WANDS
pride in self, achieving your goal

SEVEN OF CUPS
sensual excess

9 Concepts come together

• DEEP HARMONY • FAMILY • HAPPINESS • JOY • LOVE • PROTECTION • HOME

Ten of Cups

The ultimate card for a happy marriage and wonderful home life. This card radiates harmony and love from family, friends and children. Material and spiritual needs are satisfied. A sense of completion.

DESCRIPTION
A loving couple stands with arms outstretched as two children play. They face their home on the hills. A rainbow with ten cups fills the sky. This signifies the fulfilment of a promise and a sign that difficult times are over. The house symbolises safety and comfort. The green vegetation signifies fertility, and the river indicates the flow of emotion.

OVERVIEW
The Ten of Cups represents happiness and emotional fulfilment. It indicates playfulness and creativity. It can also signify reunions, home comings or family gatherings. Feeling content and at peace with the world. Something coming full circle, the completion of a cycle. This card sometimes appears after times of trouble, signifying that the storm is over.

LOVE
The Ten of Cups is an auspicious card for long-term relationships and marriage, representing a relationship filled with love and respect. It is a soulmate card. A brilliant card to draw if you want to deepen your commitment or want to have children. If you are single, the Ten of Cups can indicate the beginning of a new relationship.

CAREER
This card suggests that things are going well with your career and that your hard work is paying off. If you are considering a new project, you might be more successful if you involve family members or others who seem like family.

SPIRITUALITY
In a spiritual context, you may feel happy and positive. It indicates the completion of one cycle and the beginning of another. A time of fulfilment and promise.

ADVICE
Try to find a good balance between work and family life. Don't ignore your own needs while caring for your family. Ground your wishes in reality.

• TRUST • REUNIONS • HOMECOMINGS • FAMILY GATHERINGS • MARRIAGE

Celtic Cross Positions

1. **SIGNIFICATOR:** You are a confident, secure and happy person who enjoys giving and receiving love.

2. **OBSTACLES:** Represents strength in relationships but also the restrictions that family life can impose on a person.

3. **ROOT:** Represents a desire to settle down. Wanting a happy home or marriage.

4. **PAST:** A recent reunion or period of contentment and happiness.

5. **CROWN:** Represents joy and contentment. The family's well-being affects your happiness. Indicates love, satisfaction and fulfilment. Opportunity for growth or expansion.

6. **NEAR FUTURE:** Family gatherings and homecomings. Possible marriage or pregnancy. Indicates growth of projects and abundance in all things.

7. **FEAR:** A fear of not finding love. A fear of ending up alone.

8. **JUDGEMENT:** Represents someone who puts their family first. Someone who is dependable and can be relied on.

9. **HOPE:** Represents a wish for marriage and family. Simple joy, contentment and a sense of harmony.

10. **OUTCOME:** Represents marriage, family stability and happiness. Strong relationships and a happy home life. Abundance and fertility. A period of satisfaction, pleasure and contentment.

OPPOSING CARDS

THE DEVIL
lack of joy or peace

THE TOWER
upheaval, chaos

THREE OF SWORDS
heartbreak, loneliness

NINE OF SWORDS
anguish, sorrow, despair

TEN OF SWORDS
down in the pits, feeling victimised

REINFORCING CARDS

THE LOVERS
family relationships, bonding

THE STAR
joy, positive feelings, blessings

THE WORLD
happiness, emotional fulfilment

SIX OF CUPS
feeling blessed, happy, joyful

10 Completion, success, transformation

• NEWS • PSYCHIC GIFTS • SENSITIVITY • MOODINESS • THOUGHTFUL • IMAGINATIVE • CHILD

Page of Cups

As with all Pages, the Page of Cups signifies youthful energy and can represent either a person or a situation. Something has just begun — a new relationship, creative venture or spiritual quest. Perhaps a period of study. There could be romance or a marriage proposal.

DESCRIPTION
A youth stands on a beach, holding a cup with a fish inside. Behind him is the ocean. He wears a tunic decorated with water lilies and a blue hat. The fish symbolises spiritual wisdom, harmony and regeneration. The lilies stand for purity and peace. The rolling waves symbolise movement.

OVERVIEW
In a general context, the Page of Cups represents entering a new phase or the beginning of a great opportunity. It reminds us to trust our intuition. As the bringer of messages, you can also expect an invitation or proposal.

LOVE
If you are in a relationship, this card can represent engagements and birth. It is also a reminder to follow your heart and embrace your romantic side. If you are single, it can indicate that a new romance is on the horizon. The person will likely be sensitive, loving and imaginative. The Page of Cups can also show a relationship with a younger person.

CAREER
In a career context, the Page of Cups indicates positive news and creative energy. A successful job application or the beginning of a new project. The Page of Cups also represents being a dreamer rather than a doer. You may be drawn to a career in the arts or fashion industry.

SPIRITUALITY
In a spiritual context, the Page of Cups represents intuition and psychic abilities. Listen to your inner voice.

ADVICE
Be more sensitive to your partner's needs. Being light-hearted is fun, but sometimes it is necessary to take responsibility.

· ARTISTIC · BIRTH · DREAMS · PROPOSALS · INNER-CHILD · INTUITION · NAÏVETY

Celtic Cross Positions

1. **SIGNIFICATOR:** An intuitive, sensitive person who is prone to moodiness.

2. **OBSTACLES:** Excitement about a new relationship or project. Your willingness to jump will contribute to your self-growth and understanding of others.

3. **ROOT:** A message has caused upheaval in your life. It could be an invitation or news of someone close to you. It can also indicate a creative time and the importance of listening to your inner voice.

4. **PAST:** You are recovering from a past hurt from which you are beginning to heal. It can also refer to a daydreamer who has wasted opportunities.

5. **CROWN:** A time to use your positive attributes to move forward. Take steps to follow your dream, write that proposal, plan that holiday. Embrace the childlike nature of being naïve.

6. **NEAR FUTURE:** Represents a birth, message, or a sensitive person entering your life. New information regarding the issue might appear in your dreams.

7. **FEAR:** You fear receiving unpleasant news or being surrounded by overly emotional people.

8. **JUDGEMENT:** This represents an introverted, gentle person. Someone in touch with their inner child.

9. **HOPE:** You hope for positive news.

10. **OUTCOME:** You are entering a new phase, and life is taking you in a new direction. This could mean a new relationship, proposal, birth, exciting project or career change. Allow your intuition to guide you through this transition.

As a person, the Page of Cups signifies a child, young person, or someone who is young at heart. The person is likely to be a daydreamer, intuitive, naïve, sensitive and idealistic. This person may be interest in creative or spiritual topics. They may be a water sign (Cancer, Scorpio or Pisces).

OPPOSING CARDS

 **FIVE OF PENTACLES**
endings, loss, hard times

 **TWO OF SWORDS**
blocked feelings, painful choices

REINFORCING CARDS

 **THE FOOL**
optimism, naïvety, intuition

 **WHEEL OF FORTUNE**
change, new direction

 **THE WORLD**
change, new direction

• BEING IN LOVE • NEW OPPORTUNITIES • FRIENDSHIP • EMOTIONS

Knight of Cups

DESCRIPTION
A knight on a white horse holds out a golden cup as though carrying a message from the heart. His cloak is decorated with images of fish, symbolising spiritual wisdom, harmony and regeneration. The water in the background symbolises consciousness and creativity. His winged helmet and boots show an active imagination. The horse moves slowly, giving an air of calmness and peace. The colour white symbolises purity and spirituality.

The Knight of Cups represents both a person and a situation. If a situation, it signifies a change for the better, new opportunities and good messages. The pursuit of an idea, the realisation of dreams, the beginning of a project.

OVERVIEW
The Knight of Cups can represent proposals and invitations. It suggests that it is a good time to consider a new path, and that you should follow your dreams. It might indicate travel over water. This card signifies affection and warmth, but also hints that you are not being entirely honest about your feelings.

LOVE
If you are in a relationship, the Knight of Cups hints at proposals or an offer of a deeper commitment. It can also indicate that you need to spend some time bringing the romance back into your relationship. If you are single, the Knight of Cups suggests that love is on the horizon.

CAREER
Represents good news or an unexpected offer. The Knight brings movement, creativity and a possible new path or opportunity.

SPIRITUALITY
In a spiritual context, the Knight of Cups recommends following your intuition and increasing your psychic awareness. If you are interested in healing, now is a good time to follow this path.

ADVICE
Have you been taking things too personally? Have you been moody or emotional? The Knight suggests that you step back and look at things objectively. Perhaps you are in love with the idea of being in love and need to consider if your feelings are genuine.

• LOVE • HAPPINESS • ROMANTIC PROPOSALS • CHIVALRY • MESSAGES • CREATIVITY

Celtic Cross Positions

1. **SIGNIFICATOR:** You are emotional and impulsive. You might be so single-minded that you fail to consider the other options available.

2. **OBSTACLES:** Someone who desires to follow their heart and dreams. It awakens new and intense feelings that could be either positive or negative.

3. **ROOT:** Suggests you are thinking about your next adventure and looking for new goals. You desire movement and change.

4. **PAST:** Represents a time of activity, a high point in your life. It can also represent an important past relationship. This person may appear in your future.

5. **CROWN:** Represents feeling stuck where you are now and looking for a way out. In a relationship, you may be expected to choose between what your heart tells you and what your head says. Possibly a house move.

6. **NEAR FUTURE:** Represents the need to stay focused on your goal. You need willpower and strength to be successful. Possibly a move across water.

7. **FEAR:** You fear romance and giving yourself fully to someone.

8. **JUDGEMENT:** Represents a romantic individual who is idealistic and charming.

9. **HOPE:** Represents a hope for love and happiness or that a creative project is successful.

10. **OUTCOME:** Represents romantic proposals. A positive card for the future. Hard work will be required to be successful, but it is essential not to compromise your values.

As a person, the Knight of Cups is emotional, romantic, gentle and idealistic. He is chivalrous and a good negotiator. He may be a water sign (Cancer, Scorpio or Pisces).

REINFORCING CARDS

 **THE EMPRESS**
love, romantic proposals

 **FOUR OF WANDS**
a possible house move

 **TEN OF PENTACLES**
physical comfort

COURT CARD PAIRS

KNIGHT OF CUPS (introvert)   **QUEEN OF WANDS** (extrovert)

Knight of Cups:
- teaches the Queen about inner happiness
- annoys the Queen by obsessing about feelings

• EMPATHIC • INTUITIVE • WARMTH • POETIC • ARTISTIC • PROTECTIVE • DISTANT

Queen of Cups

The Queen of Cups represents a kind person who carries an air of calmness and sensitivity. She may appear distant and aloof. Enchantingly attractive. This card encourages you to follow your heart and creative endeavours.

OVERVIEW
In a general context, the Queen of Cups signifies a warm, loving, caring and affectionate person. Emotions are taking priority in your life right now. Can also refer to dreams and intuition.

LOVE
If you are in a relationship, this card indicates a time of caring, fulfilment and emotional security. It encourages you to be honest about your feelings. If you are single, she encourages you to go out and meet new people, as a new romance could come your way.

CAREER
This card can indicate that you would be suited to a job in a caring profession (nursing, counselling or healing) or a creative field (art or fashion). An older woman may offer you support and guidance.

SPIRITUALITY
Signifies strong intuition and psychic abilities. Pay attention to your dreams and visions.

ADVICE
This card indicates that you should be mindful of how you treat yourself. She can also suggest that you may be too sensitive.

DESCRIPTION
The Queen sits on a throne, holding a golden cup with handles shaped like angels. This cup is closed – suggesting that the Queen's feelings come from her subconscious mind. The throne is decorated with sea and fish symbols representing the unconscious. Beneath her, a river flows, representing emotion and perception. Her feet do not touch the water, suggesting she is not overwhelmed by her feelings. Cherubs adorn her chair, representing innocence.

• ALOOF • CREATIVE • ENCHANTING • LOVING • COMPASSIONATE • SENSITIVE

Celtic Cross Positions

1. **SIGNIFICATOR:** You are calm and compassionate and understand the feelings of others. You are drawn towards healing and nurturing.

2. **OBSTACLES:** You might be too emotionally involved in order to see the situation clearly. A good time to focus on a creative outlet.

3. **ROOT:** You may need to be more patient than usual to handle the current situation.

4. **PAST:** Represents an influential female in your past. Someone who was helpful on your journey – a teacher or parental figure. It can also represent a time when you were patient and understanding.

5. **CROWN:** People are drawn to you because of your kindness, patience and wisdom. This can be draining. Remember to take time for yourself.

6. **NEAR FUTURE:** Represents having to be more mature than usual, either in a caring or decision-making situation. People will look to you for advice.

7. **FEAR:** You fear letting people down, of failing in your responsibilities.

8. **JUDGEMENT:** Represents a strong feminine person with a kind and sensitive soul.

9. **HOPE:** A wish that people will take notice of you and that you will find your calling.

10. **OUTCOME:** You can expect a period of satisfaction and contentment. A time of intuition and meaningful dreams. You may need to spend time healing yourself or others.

As a person, the Queen of Cups is kind, caring and supportive. She is empathetic, loving and warm but can be shy. She is creative, artistic and intuitive. She may be a water sign (Cancer, Scorpio or Pisces).

OPPOSING CARDS

 **5 SWORDS**
dishonesty, loss, betrayal

REINFORCING CARDS

 **THE EMPRESS**
love, abundance, fertility

COURT CARD PAIRS

QUEEN OF CUPS (loving) **QUEEN OF SWORDS** (harsh)

Queen of Cups:
- teaches the Queen of Swords about love
- annoys the Queen of Swords because she is too gentle

• HONESTY • IDEALISTIC • MOODINESS • ARTISTIC • CREATIVITY • INTELLIGENCE • MATURE

King of Cups

The King of Cups represents a wise, honest and sensitive man who can be moody. He might be difficult to know and understand. Strives to control and master his emotions.

OVERVIEW
The King of Cups represents compassion, maturity and wisdom. It can indicate that you are learning to control your emotions.

LOVE
If you are in a relationship, the King of Cups is auspicious as it represents a good husband, partner or father. If you are single, you might meet someone with the qualities of this card.

CAREER
Regarding career, the King of Cups can indicate that an older male may offer you support or guidance. It can also suggest that you have the diplomacy skills and wisdom to resolve issues and create a pleasant working environment. You are well-liked and respected by your colleagues.

SPIRITUALITY
Signifies a psychic or intuitive ability. This card indicates that you may receive and understand messages sent by the spirit.

ADVICE
You may be trying to control your emotions too strongly which stops you from expressing your true feelings.

DESCRIPTION
The King wears blue and gold, the colours of authority and status. His fish amulet symbolises creativity. He holds a cup (representing emotions) and a sceptre (indicating power). He sits on a granite throne in a turbulent ocean. Behind him is a jumping fish and a ship. The King stays calm and balanced, even in rough situations, and has learned to control his emotions.

• CALM • CARING • SYMPATHETIC • WISE • TOLERANT • DIPLOMATIC • BALANCED • LOYAL

Celtic Cross Positions

1. **SIGNIFICATOR:** Your ability to understand the emotions involved gives you more choice than you realise. You need to remain level-headed and get the job done.

2. **OBSTACLES:** Stop ignoring or repressing your emotions and learn to master them. Negative feelings, such as jealousy or envy, may be clouding your vision.

3. **ROOT:** You may be called upon to give advice, but take care that your own feelings don't interfere.

4. **PAST:** Can refer to a recent relationship with someone who shares qualities with the King. Can also signify you or a situation. Perhaps you were called upon to be a mediator or acted with maturity instead of an emotional outburst.

5. **CROWN:** You might connect with someone who can help you immensely.

6. **NEAR FUTURE:** You may need to make a tough decision. Think things over and try to make a mature choice.

7. **FEAR:** You might be afraid of making decisions or expressing your opinion.

8. **JUDGEMENT:** Represents a wise older person who is emotionally mature.

9. **HOPE:** Represents a desire to be in control.

10. **OUTCOME:** A positive, peaceful outcome. You are possibly doing well and feeling as though you are in control. If a decision needs to be made, choose wisely.

As a person, the King of Cups is caring, affectionate, diplomatic and empathetic. He gives sound advice and acts as a calming influence. He is focused on emotions rather than material wealth. He may be a water sign (Cancer, Scorpio or Pisces).

OPPOSING CARDS

 **FIVE OF WANDS**
petty arguments, conflict

REINFORCING CARDS

 **THE MAGICIAN**
creativity, intelligence

COURT CARD PAIRS

KING OF CUPS (tolerant)   **KING OF SWORDS** (impatient)

King of Cups:
- teaches the King of Swords to embrace mercy
- annoys the King of Swords by being too forgiving

The Suit of Pentacles

The Suit of Pentacles deals with health, finances and career. It focuses on the earthy aspects of material security, business, security and money.

If there are many Pentacles in a reading, you are likely seeking solutions to material conflicts, financial matters or concerns with career and work.

The negative side of Pentacles includes being overly materialistic, possessive, stubborn or greedy.

Element: Earth

Keywords: money, possessions, materialism, wealth, resistance, stability

Corresponding playing card suit: Diamonds

Astrological signs: Taurus, Virgo and Capricorn

Noted for: finances, growth, nature

Ace of Pentacles

beginnings, opportunities

Two of Pentacles

balancing act

Three of Pentacles

skills, recognition

Four of Pentacles

materialism, stinginess

Five of Pentacles

poverty, hardship

Six of Pentacles

charity, generosity

Seven of Pentacles

evaluation, harvest

Eight of Pentacles

training, achievement

Nine of Pentacles

self-assured, confident

Ten of Pentacles

prosperity, security

Page of Pentacles

news, opportunities

Knight of Pentacles

patient, dependable

Queen of Pentacles

generous, independent

King of Pentacles

wealthy, good leader

• NEW BEGINNING • MATERIAL GAIN • BUSINESS OPPORTUNITIES • PROSPERITY • REWARD FOR EFFORT

Ace of Pentacles

The Ace of Pentacles represents new beginnings, material abundance and improving finances. It indicates that you are likely to be successful in business endeavours. It bodes well for financial rewards and security.

OVERVIEW
This Ace represents new beginnings and prosperity, the beginning of something successful. This card brings feelings of positivity, inspiration and energy. It also signifies abundance in all areas of life. This is the time to achieve your goals and realise your potential.

LOVE
If you are currently in a relationship, this Ace offers stability, peace and a grounded love. It encourages you to bring some excitement into your relationship, especially if things feel stagnant. It can also indicate an engagement or marriage. If you are single, this card's energy of new beginnings is a good omen.

CAREER
The Ace of Pentacles represents a positive new beginning, getting that job, promotion or other opportunity you've been hoping for. If you work for yourself, this Ace suggests that your plans will work out. Now is a good time to launch a business venture or project.

SPIRITUALITY
This card offers exciting possibilities and suggests that you try something new. The fresh energy of this card will motivate and inspire you.

ADVICE
This card warns of the possibility of becoming greedy.

DESCRIPTION
A cupped hand in the clouds offers a large coin to whoever wants to take it. In the background lies a beautiful garden with red roses growing over an archway. The arch represents a passage, moving from one stage to another. The mountain peaks are mysterious, warning of hard work and challenges ahead, but also offer a fresh perspective.

• CAREER BOOST • GOOD FORTUNE • FINANCIAL SECURITY • NEW JOB • ABUNDANCE

Celtic Cross Positions

1. **SIGNIFICATOR:** You are feeling positive, inspired and ready to tackle whatever comes your way.

2. **OBSTACLES:** It is a good time to start that project that's been on your mind. Focus more on the material aspects of your life.

3. **ROOT:** Don't be led astray by emotions or fantasy. You need to be grounded in order to turn your ideas into something tangible.

4. **PAST:** Your life has recently taken a positive turn. A career change or decision that still has an impact on your life.

5. **CROWN:** You are excited about a new idea. As you become more successful, remember to help those around you.

6. **NEAR FUTURE:** You can expect a time of good fortune in your endeavours. An investor may appear, or you might get a positive response on a job application. Luck is with you, so be bold.

7. **FEAR:** You fear failure, material loss and financial insecurity.

8. **JUDGEMENT:** Represents a successful person who appears lucky in wealth and career.

9. **HOPE:** A wish for good fortune and a career change.

10. **OUTCOME:** A good luck card. Positive, creative energy. New beginnings, a new job, or a material goal will be achieved. Financial security or windfall. Realistic plans are very likely to succeed.

OPPOSING CARDS

THE DEVIL
oppression, hostility

FOUR OF SWORDS
rest, retreat

REINFORCING CARDS

THE SUN
abundance, happiness

NINE OF CUPS
prosperity, realising dreams

ACE-ACE PAIRS

An Ace-Ace pair shows that a new spirit is entering your life. It draws on the energy of the Ace of Pentacles (prosperity, abundance, trust, security), plus one of these:

ACE OF CUPS
deep feelings, intimacy, compassion, love

ACE OF SWORDS
intelligence, reason, justice, truth, clarity

ACE OF WANDS
creativity, excitement, adventure, courage

1 Beginning

• BALANCE • RESOURCEFULNESS • UPS AND DOWNS • ADAPTABILITY • FLEXIBILITY

Two of Pentacles

The Two of Pentacles represents the balancing or juggling of more than one aspect of our lives. Although balance is necessary, this card also reminds us to have fun and stay flexible.

OVERVIEW
This card can indicate that you are trying to maintain the balance between various aspects of your life. It represents the ups and downs that come our way and suggests that you are adaptable and flexible enough to get through them. This card can also warn against juggling too many things at once – its presence can indicate that decisions need to be made.

LOVE
If you are in a relationship, you and your partner might need to make a big decision. It could also indicate that you are not giving your partner the attention they deserve. If you are single, this card suggests that you might not have the time or energy to dedicate to a new relationship right now.

CAREER
The Two of Pentacles can signify a decision that needs to be made. This card advises that you focus on fewer things rather than juggling too many different tasks.

SPIRITUALITY
Spiritually, this card indicates that you are juggling too many ideas and are not progressing.

ADVICE
This card suggests that balance is missing from your life. It can also indicate that you need to take financial responsibility.

DESCRIPTION
A man dances as he juggles two pentacles. One is held above the other, signifying that one is more important. The cloth he juggles with is shaped like the infinity symbol, suggesting he can handle unlimited problems. Two ships ride the ups and downs of life. The man is concentrating, yet doesn't seem concerned with the turbulent sea behind him, and dances despite it.

• JUGGLING TASKS OR FINANCES • PROFIT AND LOSS • FINANCIAL DECISIONS • BALANCING ACT

Celtic Cross Positions

1. **SIGNIFICATOR:** You appear to juggle all your responsibilities seamlessly.

2. **OBSTACLES:** You have difficulty in finding balance. Managing everything required of you may lead to feelings of exhaustion.

3. **ROOT:** You juggle all demands made of you, which can drain the fun out of life. Make time to enjoy yourself.

4. **PAST:** Represents a past moment of change and adaptation. You may have moved locations or grown as a person.

5. **CROWN:** You are balancing several aspects of your life such as work and play, family and friends.

6. **NEAR FUTURE:** You will be required to juggle several responsibilities in order to stay on top of things. Try to find balance and incorporate ways to have fun.

7. **FEAR:** You fear that you will not manage the challenges that lie ahead.

8. **JUDGEMENT:** Others see you as capable of handling life's ups and downs. Able to multi-task and work under pressure.

9. **HOPE:** You hope to overcome every hurdle necessary to reach your goal.

10. **OUTCOME:** A choice needs to be made as you cannot indefinitely juggle so many responsibilities. Others must step up and share the load. Energetic and joyful moments lie ahead if you can remain flexible and playful and let go of some unnecessary burdens.

OPPOSING CARDS

THE HIEROPHANT
following the program, being conventional

FIVE OF WANDS
being at cross-purposes, not working out

FOUR OF SWORDS
rest, quiet, low activity

SIX OF SWORDS
the blues, feeling listless

REINFORCING CARDS

TEMPERANCE
balance, finding the right mix

FOUR OF WANDS
fun, excitement, parties

TWO OF PENTACLES
juggling activities

2 Duality, balance, harmony, reflection

• PROMOTION • GROWTH • SKILLS • RECOGNITION • ACHIEVEMENT • MATERIAL INCREASE

Three of Pentacles

The Three of Pentacles shows the rewards of hard work and good skills. It implies that the initial stages of a venture have been successfully completed. It symbolises teamwork, promotion or a raise.

OVERVIEW
The Three of Pentacles signifies hard work, dedication, and commitment. It also represents working well with others and a solid partnership. It indicates that a business endeavour has a good foundation and is filled with the possibility of success.

LOVE
If you are in a relationship, this card indicates that you are committed and put effort into the relationship. If you are single, the Three of Pentacles can suggest that you have attracted someone's attention.

CAREER
An incredibly auspicious card to draw in a career reading. The Three of Pentacles indicates that you are working on something you are passionate about. It suggests being rewarded for hard work. Teamwork and partnerships can lead to success. Your work is valued and appreciated, and you may get promoted. You may be studying or will decide to enrol in a course.

SPIRITUALITY
In a spiritual context, the Three of Pentacles indicates that you may find inspiration in old stories and myths. It also suggests working with others, joining a group or connecting spiritually with someone.

ADVICE
Are you obsessing with the details of a project and not looking at it objectively? Are you too dependent on the approval of others?

DESCRIPTION
A stonemason is working on a cathedral. In front of him, two architects hold the design plans. The ceilings and engravings signify that both parties are skilled in their respective crafts. The stonemason appears to be discussing his progress with the architects. Their body language shows their mutual respect.

• TEAM SPIRIT • APPRENTICESHIP • PLANNING • GROWTH • HARD WORK • COMMITMENT

Celtic Cross Positions

1. **SIGNIFICATOR:** You are proud of what you have achieved. You have worked hard to reach this point and are not afraid to ask for advice.

2. **OBSTACLES:** Represents the need for teamwork and cooperation. Consider including others in your project.

3. **ROOT:** A time for hard work and cooperation. Perhaps studying to increase your knowledge or branching off into an entirely new field. Dedication and hard work are required.

4. **PAST:** Represents a period of intense study and hard work that has brought you to the current position.

5. **CROWN:** Reaching out to others has a positive effect all around and could add value to the service you provide.

6. **NEAR FUTURE:** Your hard work pays off. You receive recognition for your efforts. You might need to consider teamwork.

7. **FEAR:** You fear asking for help or are afraid of disappointing others.

8. **JUDGEMENT:** Represents a capable, hard-working person.

9. **HOPE:** Represents a hope for promotion or recognition.

10. **OUTCOME:** Your business venture is destined for success. You have planned and worked with others for the best possible outcome. You have the necessary skills and knowledge to take things to the next level.

OPPOSING CARDS

FIVE OF WANDS
lack of teamwork, no cooperation

SEVEN OF WANDS
opposition, dissension

EIGHT OF SWORDS
not feeling up to the job, lacking direction

NINE OF PENTACLES
doing it yourself, not focusing on teamwork

REINFORCING CARDS

THE HIEROPHANT
working in a team or group

TEMPERANCE
combining forces

THREE OF WANDS
planning, preparing for the future

THREE OF CUPS
working in a group

3 Trio, planning, ideas, creation

• SECURITY • SOLID FOUNDATION • STABILITY • MATERIALISM • RESISTANCE TO CHANGE • STAGNATION

Four of Pentacles

The Four of Pentacles represents material stability and clinging to your wealth. You are sitting on a solid foundation and don't want to risk this by taking chances.

OVERVIEW
In a general context, the Four of Pentacles can indicate that you are holding on to people, possessions, ideals, situations or past issues. Perhaps there are deep-seated issues that you need to let go of. This card also suggests that you are consumed by financial affairs and are allowing yourself to become miserly.

LOVE
This card can indicate possessiveness, jealousy or controlling behaviour. If you are single, you might be holding onto feelings for someone and are not ready to move on.

CAREER
In a career spread, the Four of Pentacles indicates that you are in a stable position due to hard work. Don't let fear of losing this make you paranoid and wary of sharing with others. This could take the form of being possessive of your clients or unwilling to share ideas with co-workers.

SPIRITUALITY
Holding onto the past might be restricting your ability to progress along a spiritual path.

ADVICE
Be aware of controlling and possessive behaviour – either from yourself or someone else. Don't allow greed to limit your potential for growth.

DESCRIPTION
A man sits on a stool, a town lies in the distance. He clutches a coin as though afraid of losing it. Another is balanced on his head, negatively affecting his connection with spirit and holding him down. He has two more underneath his feet, so he can't move without losing them. By clinging to his coins in this way, he limits his movement. He is alone. Everyone else is in the town behind him. He is so fixated on keeping his wealth safe that he doesn't realise what's been lost.

• CLINGING TO POSSESSIONS • WEALTH • HOARDING • STINGINESS • CONTROL

Celtic Cross Positions

1. **SIGNIFICATOR:** You are clinging to your resources and allow material objects to have too much power over you.

2. **OBSTACLES:** You are in a position of stalemate caused by miserliness or greed.

3. **ROOT:** You are being stubborn and resisting change. It might be best to stop clinging and let go.

4. **PAST:** Your current situation is likely caused by holding onto something material or being stingy with money.

5. **CROWN:** You need to let go of the past in order to move forward in a positive way, even if it is difficult or painful. You may reconnect with something from your past, possibly a material item.

6. **NEAR FUTURE:** You may soon experience a sense of security through material goods and finances. A warning not to give it too much importance.

7. **FEAR:** You fear change or losing wealth and possessions.

8. **JUDGEMENT:** Represents a stubborn person, who holds on to material things. Someone who is controlling and possessive.

9. **HOPE:** A desire to be financially independent and in control.

10. **OUTCOME:** Security and a solid foundation on which to build your future. Your desire to control and keep things the same may prevent personal growth.

OPPOSING CARDS

THE FOOL
spontaneous, impulsive

THE EMPRESS
open-hearted, generous

WHEEL OF FORTUNE
movement, rapid change

THE HANGED MAN
letting go, not trying to control

SIX OF WANDS
popular, loves people

REINFORCING CARDS

THE EMPEROR
control, order, structure

THE CHARIOT
control

TWO OF SWORDS
stalemate, blockage

TEN OF PENTACLES
stability, wealth, solid foundation

4 Stability, order, making things happen

• WORRY • UNEMPLOYMENT • HARD TIMES • FINANCIAL LOSS • LONELINESS • ANXIETY

Five of Pentacles

The Five of Pentacles represents loss, poverty and insecurities. As with all the fives in the Tarot, it is a difficult card. It can represent poor health, material and economic loss, and rejection.

OVERVIEW
In a general context, the Five of Pentacles represents hardship, rejection or an adverse change in circumstances. It can signify a wide range of difficulties. It can also indicate that you feel lost, hopeless and unworthy.

LOVE
If you are in a relationship, you may be struggling with feeling ignored. You might be putting the relationship at risk because you are not giving your partner attention. If you are single, the Five of Pentacles can indicate feeling rejected. It can also represent the difficulties of being a single parent.

CAREER
In a career spread, the Five of Pentacles can represent unemployment, job losses or going out of business. Alternatively, you may feel trapped in your job but hopeless about changing your situation.

SPIRITUALITY
You may be going through a tough time spiritually. You are likely feeling lost or drained. Hardships often show us our strengths, so embrace any lessons.

ADVICE
Often, our own attitude prevents us from moving forward. The Five of Pentacles reminds us that help is available for those seeking solutions. Don't be so consumed by your problems that you fail to see when help is offered.

DESCRIPTION
Two people walk through the icy wind and snow, looking very downtrodden and out of luck. One is injured and on crutches, while the other is barefoot and has only a thin blanket for protection against the bleak winter weather. Behind them is a brightly lit church that radiates warmth. It is a symbol of hope, faith, and spiritual support. However, because the two people are so focused on their situation, they fail to see that help is available.

• STRAIN • STRUGGLE • SUFFERING • BAD LUCK • POVERTY • BREAKUPS • SCANDAL • DISGRACE

Celtic Cross Positions

1. **SIGNIFICATOR:** You may be going through hardship and are feeling uninspired and unmotivated.

2. **OBSTACLES:** You possibly feel alienated due to your attitudes or beliefs and are ignoring the help that is being offered.

3. **ROOT:** Don't allow yourself to be consumed with worry. There is always a solution. Consider reaching out to others who might be able to offer guidance.

4. **PAST:** Represents a past time when you were poor or felt alienated. It was a difficult time, but you've learned your lessons and have moved on.

5. **CROWN:** Comfort is close at hand if you choose to look for it.

6. **NEAR FUTURE:** A difficult time, a struggle you must overcome. Keep your eyes and heart open. Help can be found in the most unexpected places.

7. **FEAR:** Represents fear of not being accepted and experiencing material hardship and financial loss.

8. **JUDGEMENT:** Represents someone going through a difficult time and losing hope.

9. **HOPE:** Represents the desire for warmth and success.

10. **OUTCOME:** A struggle lies ahead. You need to change how you live your life and make decisions to guide it in a different direction. You may find help in unexpected places if you open up to opportunities and accept assistance.

OPPOSING CARDS

STRENGTH
strength, stamina

TEMPERANCE
good health

THE SUN
vitality, strong constitution

SIX OF WANDS
acclaim, recognition

SEVEN OF PENTACLES
material reward

REINFORCING CARDS

THE TOWER
hard times

TEN OF WANDS
struggling to make ends meet, hard times

FIVE OF CUPS
rejection, loss of support and approval

THREE OF SWORDS
rejection, separation, lack of support

5 Adaptation, challenge, conflict

• INVESTMENTS • CHARITY • BONUS • GIFTS • PROSPERITY • JUSTICE • DIVIDENDS

Six of Pentacles

The Six of Pentacles represents generosity and giving or receiving gifts or money. The standing figure on the card has the power to change the lives of the beggars, and his scale tells us that he decides who receives and who doesn't. A card of power and control.

OVERVIEW
The Six of Pentacles can signify equality and being valued or rewarded. You might receive money owed to you. If you are doing financially well, it is a reminder to share your fortune. A strong sense of community support; you might be called upon to help others. If you are in need, you may receive help from others.

LOVE
If you are in a relationship, this card indicates generosity and sharing between you and your partner. If you are single, the Six of Pentacles can suggest that you will meet someone kind-hearted. Being generous (with your time, money or energy) may lead to meeting someone new.

CAREER
A great card if you are job hunting or considering a career change. This card indicates that you might receive the approval you seek from someone in a powerful position. If you run a business, this card can symbolise attracting investors.

SPIRITUALITY
In a spiritual context, this card suggests being generous with your knowledge and sharing your spiritual experiences. You may also be on the receiving end and learn from someone else.

ADVICE
When this card appears, you are either in the position of giving or are dependent on the kindness of someone else. It can urge you to be more cautious about where you spend your time, money and energy. It can also suggest that you have not been generous enough.

DESCRIPTION
A prominent man handing out coins. Two beggars kneel at his feet. The man holds a scale, representing fairness and equality. Using these scales, the man decides who is worthy to receive and who is not. The beggars look at him with admiration and are entirely at the mercy of his generosity.

• GENEROSITY • ASSISTANCE • SUPPORT • SHARING • KINDNESS • AUTHORITY

Celtic Cross Positions

1. **SIGNIFICATOR:** You are kind, generous and fair. Someone others can turn to when they are in need.

2. **OBSTACLES:** Money has an influence on the situation. Having too much or too little changes many aspects of life.

3. **ROOT:** A time of uncertainty. Make sure your generosity does not leave you feeling depleted. You'll need your strength for what lies ahead.

4. **PAST:** Past generosity. Someone may have given you a great opportunity to which you feel indebted. Alternatively, someone might owe you money.

5. **CROWN:** Fairness and balance govern the situation. Being generous with your time, energy, and love can make a huge difference in someone's life.

6. **NEAR FUTURE:** Expect good job prospects, receiving money owed or approval from someone you deem important.

7. **FEAR:** You fear being dependent on someone else's generosity.

8. **JUDGEMENT:** A generous person who is willing to lift others up.

9. **HOPE:** You feel that you are entitled to certain rewards for your hard work and hope to receive acknowledgement of this.

10. **OUTCOME:** Suggests that you'll be successful in your endeavours. You may find yourself in a position to help others or make a difference in someone else's life.

OPPOSING CARDS

TEN OF WANDS
struggling to make ends meet, hard times

FIVE OF PENTACLES
lack, not having

REINFORCING CARDS

THE EMPRESS
abundance, physical comfort

THE WORLD
affluence, material fulfilment

SEVEN OF PENTACLES
material reward, having

TEN OF PENTACLES
affluence, having

 Patterns, togetherness

• ASSESS AND EVALUATE • PAUSE IN BUSINESS PROJECT • REST • WEIGH OPTIONS

Seven of Pentacles

The Seven of Pentacles represents taking a break after a period of hard work. It can represent being at a crossroads and taking stock of what you have achieved, before deciding on a plan for the future.

OVERVIEW
The Seven of Pentacles indicates that you have worked hard and can now take a moment to enjoy the fruits of your labour. It implies that you have made progress, but much work still lies ahead. However, you can feel satisfied with your achievements and abilities.

LOVE
If you are in a relationship, this card suggests that it is nurturing and fulfilling. It also can indicate pregnancy. If you are single, it suggests that you may be taking stock to decide what you really want.

CAREER
This card indicates that your hard work has started to pay off. You have achieved your current goal and can now focus your energy on the future. You should not take your talents for granted and should always look at new ways of using them. The Seven of Pentacles can also suggest that someone is nearing retirement.

SPIRITUALITY
In a spiritual context, this card indicates that your spiritual development has been achieved by hard work.

ADVICE
This card reminds you not to overdo it and deplete yourself. It is important to pause in order to review the situation and make sure that things are going in the direction you intended. A reminder not to place too much importance on material wealth.

DESCRIPTION
A man leans on his hoe, gazing down at a plant growing pentacles. The plant and pentacles represent the fruits of his labour. Although he looks tired, he is proud of his achievements and success. He has worked hard.

• OBJECTIVE VIEW • HARD WORK PAYING OFF • HARVEST • REWARDS • PROFITS • RESULTS

Celtic Cross Positions

1. **SIGNIFICATOR:** You are a hard worker and have achieved a great deal. You might be at a crossroads as you try to figure out your way forward.

2. **OBSTACLES:** Represents weighing different decisions, or feeling emotionally and physically exhausted.

3. **ROOT:** Life is slow and steady, and you enjoy the rewards of hard work.

4. **PAST:** Past hard work has led to the current situation. You may be feeling drained or depleted. You might also be confused about which path to follow.

5. **CROWN:** You might feel stuck in a situation. This card suggests you'll remain in this position for a while.

6. **NEAR FUTURE:** Represents continued growth. Expect your current focus to thrive – whether it's a new venture, job, relationship, hobby or friendship. Hard work will be required to maintain success, so keep working.

7. **FEAR:** You fear working too hard and failing.

8. **JUDGEMENT:** A hard-working individual who is forward-thinking, practical and steadfast.

9. **HOPE:** You hope for success and that all your hard work will be worth it.

10. **OUTCOME:** A positive outcome. A reward for your past efforts. A possible decision to be made. Indicates that one phase is over, and this is a time for rest and recovery before the next phase begins.

OPPOSING CARDS

WHEEL OF FORTUNE
movement, action, direction change

EIGHT OF WANDS
rapid action

FIVE OF PENTACLES
lack of reward, hardship

REINFORCING CARDS

THE EMPRESS
material reward

JUSTICE
assessing where you are, deciding a course

JUDGEMENT
decision point

FOUR OF SWORDS
rest, thinking things over

NINE OF WANDS
pause in work to rest

7. Accomplishments, self-expansion

• TRAINING • ACHIEVEMENT • SATISFACTION • SELF-EMPLOYMENT • NEW CAREER

Eight of Pentacles

The Eight of Pentacles represents the skill, dedication and hard work needed to get a job done properly. It reminds us that the more we put in, the more we get out. A new work or training opportunity may be coming your way.

OVERVIEW
The Eight of Pentacles represents a time of hard work and dedication. You may be learning a new skill, improving an existing talent, or working hard at a business. This card suggests that your efforts will be rewarded and encourages you to believe in yourself and to keep going.

LOVE
If you are in a relationship, this card indicates that it has a solid foundation. If you are single, the Eight of Pentacles suggests that good things will come if you remain true to yourself.

CAREER
In the career context, this card an excellent omen. Training opportunities, new business clients, and a steady work flow are all options. Focus your energy and skill on the task at hand, and don't get distracted by things that are less important.

SPIRITUALITY
This card suggests that you have been gaining spiritual knowledge and skills.

ADVICE
Avoid getting into a rut by changing your routines. Consider expanding your horizons by learning a new skill or improving an existing one.

DESCRIPTION
A young man engraves eight coins. In the background lies a small town. However, he has separated himself from distractions to focus fully on the task at hand. He is concentrating, eager to do a good job and avoid mistakes. His skills improve as he progresses.

• SUCCESS • DEDICATION • TRADE • REPUTATION • CRAFTSMANSHIP • QUALITY • KNOWLEDGE

Celtic Cross Positions

1. **SIGNIFICATOR:** You are a hard-working person on the path to success. You understand the importance of delivering a high standard of work. You may not always get the recognition you deserve.

2. **OBSTACLES:** If you have been distracted lately, get back your work focus. Organise your workspace to be more efficient.

3. **ROOT:** Represents steady, focused and consistent work. A reminder to balance work with the other important things in your life.

4. **PAST:** Represents a time of hard work and focus, and a pause before the next phase begins.

5. **CROWN:** A time of focus, concentration and hard work.

6. **NEAR FUTURE:** Represents steady work in your future. Your skills are well-known and will keep you busy.

7. **FEAR:** You fear distraction and losing your reputation.

8. **JUDGEMENT:** Represents a hard-working, dependable person who is steadfast and focused.

9. **HOPE:** You desire to work for yourself or with your hands. A willingness to learn and broaden your horizons.

10. **OUTCOME:** Your hard work will pay off. You will successfully complete your project if you remain dedicated. The creation of something significant and positive.

OPPOSING CARDS

FOUR OF CUPS
lacking interest, not caring, apathetic

SEVEN OF CUPS
lazy, lacking drive

REINFORCING CARDS

THE MAGICIAN
focus, concentration

THE HIEROPHANT
learning, studying

NINE OF WANDS
keeping at it, persistence

8 Inspiration, structure, balance

• PRIDE • SUCCESS • PLEASURE • CONFIDENCE • ACCOMPLISHMENT • PEACE

Nine of Pentacles

The Nine of Pentacles represents luxury, financial security and self-confidence. Someone who has worked hard and achieved a great deal. A time for enjoying the rewards that come from hard work.

OVERVIEW
The Nine of Pentacles represents success, financial wealth, independence and freedom. You have worked hard to create the luxury and security that you are now enjoying. This card tells you to feel proud as you have accomplished your goal.

LOVE
This card suggests that if you are in a relationship, it is stable and offers security. If you are single, it can suggest that you enjoy the freedom and independence this offers.

CAREER
The Nine of Pentacles indicates financial success and triumph through hard work and dedication. Perhaps a promotion or bonus is on its way. If you are in business, this card suggests successful endeavours.

SPIRITUALITY
This card indicates that you are entering a phase of insight and wisdom on your spiritual quest.

ADVICE
Financial independence creates a sense of freedom. How free are you? Spend time figuring out what truly matters to you.

DESCRIPTION
A woman stands in a garden wearing a white gown, which represents purity. The flower pattern symbolises glory. The red on her clothing indicates that she is passionate about what she does. The grapes and coins represent her accomplishments. Her hand rests upon one of the coins, indicating that she has a healthy relationship with money. She is enjoying the fruits of her labour. A hooded falcon signifies her freedom of spirit. The large house in the background also hints at her financial success.

• SELF-ASSURED • STABILITY • WEALTH • INHERITANCE • INDEPENDENCE • FINANCIAL SECURITY

Celtic Cross Positions

1. **SIGNIFICATOR:** You are self-confident, self-assured, financially independent. Possibly a loner.

2. **OBSTACLES:** You are involved in a lonely task that requires patience and persistence. You need to resist temptation and stay focused.

3. **ROOT:** Represents the ability to show restraint and self-control in order to achieve your goals. Temporary sacrifice for long-term gain. Represents the need to take matters into your own hands.

4. **PAST:** You have worked hard for your success. It could also represent a spoiled childhood or a recent house move.

5. **CROWN:** You have stability, independence and financial security.

6. **NEAR FUTURE:** An auspicious time in which you can enjoy the things you've worked for. If you have recently been going through a difficult time, this card indicates that things will soon improve.

7. **FEAR:** You fear being dependent on others.

8. **JUDGEMENT:** Represents a self-reliant person who doesn't easily accept the help offered by others. Someone who prefers to be alone and in control.

9. **HOPE:** You hope to be self-reliant and successful.

10. **OUTCOME:** Suggests that you will be successful and achieve what you hope to. Financial success, happiness and pleasure.

OPPOSING CARDS

THE EMPRESS
earthy sensuality

SEVEN OF CUPS
being undisciplined, self-indulgent

THREE OF PENTACLES
working in a team

REINFORCING CARDS

THE CHARIOT
self-control, discipline

SEVEN OF SWORDS
relying on yourself, acting on your own

9 Concepts come together

• PROSPERITY • SECURITY • STABILITY • SUCCESS • FAMILY FINANCES • PROPERTY

Ten of Pentacles

The Ten of Pentacles represents financial security and a stable family life. Reaching a stage where you have everything you want. The fulfilment of your desires.

OVERVIEW
The Ten of Pentacles represents solid foundations, financial security and happiness. It also represents family responsibilities and ancestry. This card can suggest embracing traditions and upholding family values. It can also signify making an investment, such as buying a house.

LOVE
If you are in a relationship that has had difficulties lately, this card indicates that things will soon improve. Your relationship might be heading to the next stage (such as living together or engagement). If you are single, the Ten of Pentacles can indicate a new love.

CAREER
In a career context, this card suggests that you have made a good investment, have worked hard, and are enjoying prosperity. You may have created a legacy that future generations can enjoy. It can also indicate a family business.

SPIRITUALITY
This card indicates feeling spiritual satisfaction and being at peace with the world.

ADVICE
Do you allow people into your life, or have you built a wall around yourself? Opening up and sharing will add another dimension to your life.

DESCRIPTION
An older man in an embroidered robe sits with two white dogs at his feet. They symbolise loyalty and protection. A couple with a child are nearby. The wealthy man has been successful in life and enjoys sharing his wealth with his family. Traditional values are respected and upheld.

• FULFILMENT • PARENTAGE • SOLID FOUNDATIONS • ANCESTRY • INHERITANCE • WEALTH

Celtic Cross Positions

1. **SIGNIFICATOR:** You are successful, family-orientated and add value to others. Your work may send you on a personal journey or lead to inner searching.

2. **OBSTACLES:** It may be time to build a more structured lifestyle.

3. **ROOT:** You have a solid foundation and are headed towards success. You may feel vulnerable and afraid of losing what you have worked so hard to achieve.

4. **PAST:** Refers to a stage in your life when you were prosperous or happy. This still affects you. Perhaps you miss what you had.

5. **CROWN:** Following traditional methods will be helpful in achieving your goal or resolving the issue.

6. **NEAR FUTURE:** Indicates that things will go well. It is likely your current project will be successful. Look to family members for advice. A possible house move.

7. **FEAR:** You fear financial insecurity, commitment and vulnerability.

8. **JUDGEMENT:** Represents a financially secure person with a happy family.

9. **HOPE:** You hope for satisfaction, wealth, comfort and family.

10. **OUTCOME:** An auspicious outcome. It represents all forms of success – a loving family, a successful business and inner happiness. A period of satisfaction and contentment.

OPPOSING CARDS

TWO OF WANDS
being original, avoiding convention

THREE OF WANDS
exploring, going into untested areas

FIVE OF PENTACLES
hard times, material lack

REINFORCING CARDS

THE EMPRESS
affluence, luxury, physical comfort

THE HIEROPHANT
conforming, following rules, conservative

THE LOVERS
permanent unions, family ties

THE WORLD
affluence, material fulfilment

FOUR OF PENTACLES
enjoying the status quo, conserving

10 Completion, success, transformation

• CONFIDENT • PRACTICAL • DELIBERATE • METHODICAL • PROGRESS • DILIGENT • GOOD NEWS

Page of Pentacles

DESCRIPTION
A young man stands in a grassy field of flowers. The colour of his clothing suggests his connection to the element of earth, and that he is grounded and capable. In the distance are trees and a ploughed field, promising an abundant harvest. The mountain range signifies the upcoming challenges. The Page focuses completely on the gold coin that he holds.

As with all Pages, the Page of Pentacles can represent a person or a situation. Something has just begun — a new opportunity, an exciting offer or receiving exciting news. New ideas, scholarships or a business opportunity.

OVERVIEW
The Page of Pentacles is the bearer of good news in money, business, education, property or health. This card tells you to decide what you want and find an opportunity to pursue it. If you are considering starting a business or embarking on a course of study, now is a good time.

LOVE
If you are in a relationship, this card indicates loyalty and faithfulness. If you are single, perhaps you'll meet someone who embodies the characteristics of this Page – responsible, capable and practical. This card radiates new experiences, so if you are looking for love, put yourself out there and mingle with people.

CAREER
The Page of Pentacles is an auspicious card for a career reading. It tells you to look for opportunities and to expect movement in your career. New ideas, opportunities and projects are on the horizon. A reminder to be realistic about expectations and to stay grounded.

SPIRITUALITY
Indicates that you might be considering a new spiritual path or working on your divination skills. Meditation and pathworking.

ADVICE
When planning a new venture, consider your limitations beforehand and find ways to turn them into something positive.

• SOLID BEGINNINGS • SETTING GOALS • NEW PROJECTS • PLANNING • FOCUS

Celtic Cross Positions

1. **SIGNIFICATOR:** You are a capable and efficient person with big plans. A new project or venture has become your focus.

2. **OBSTACLES:** A new cycle is beginning. The wheels are already in motion. Look for opportunities and stay focused.

3. **ROOT:** Achieving your dreams is possible if you are practical, methodical and diligent in your approach.

4. **PAST:** A recent phase when you were driven and focused and experienced a taste of what you wanted from life.

5. **CROWN:** Things are going to change for the better. Good news is on its way. The potential for growth energises the situation.

6. **NEAR FUTURE:** A practical plan is being implemented. Turning dreams into reality. New beginnings. A possible course of study. If life has been difficult, it might be turning around soon.

7. **FEAR:** You are afraid of stagnating and remaining in the same position.

8. **JUDGEMENT:** Represents a loyal and steadfast person. Practical but full of ideas and new plans.

9. **HOPE:** You hope to find an opportunity to fulfil your dreams.

10. **OUTCOME:** A new phase is starting, and you can expect positive news. If you've recently taken a test, good results are likely. The beginning of a successful venture.

As a person, the Page of Pentacles is a young person, child or person who is young at heart, grounded, loyal, responsible, realistic and ambitious. Someone you can trust. They may be an Earth sign (Taurus, Virgo or Capricorn).

OPPOSING CARDS

 **KNIGHT OF WANDS** impulsive, impatient

 **TWO OF SWORDS** holding back, stagnation

REINFORCING CARDS

 **ACE OF CUPS** good news, new beginnings

 **EIGHT OF PENTACLES** diligence, methodical

 **TWO OF WANDS** planning, setting goals

• TRADITIONAL • PATIENT • TRUSTWORTHY • DEPENDABLE • STEADFAST

Knight of Pentacles

DESCRIPTION
The Knight sits on a horse, looking at the gold coin in his hand. He is in no hurry. His horse stands still. The Knight is assessing and creating a plan before he takes further action. In the background is a ploughed field, symbolising that he is willing to do the work required, even if it is repetitive.

The Knight of Pentacles can either indicate a person or a situation. The card represents patience, practicality and being grounded. The Knight is creating foundations through practical hard work. He can be considered dull because he isn't spontaneous and doesn't take chances.

OVERVIEW
The Knight of Pentacles represents responsibility, practicality, and working hard for what you want. The Knight is ambitious and achieves his goals through perseverance and determination. It can also represent being environmentally aware and an animal lover. If you are practical and capable, this card is a good omen for success.

LOVE
If you are in a relationship, this indicates it is committed. It can also suggest that the relationship has become boring. If you are single, the Knight of Pentacles suggests that your expectations for a future partner are inflexible. It can also suggest that you hold back your true feelings and avoid getting emotionally involved.

CAREER
You are ambitious and driven and likely to achieve your career goals. Your hard work will pay off. You are likely to be skilled with your hands. Not a good time act on a whim. Rather stick to traditional methods.

SPIRITUALITY
If you are feeling in a rut, try to bring some excitement and spontaneity into your spiritually practice.

ADVICE
Are you dependable and steadfast, or have you become boring and dull? Perhaps you need to stop taking yourself so seriously and have some fun.

• PRACTICAL • FAITHFUL • RESPONSIBLE • HARD WORKING • PRODUCTIVE

Celtic Cross Positions

1. **SIGNIFICATOR:** You are willing to work hard. You are practical but can be emotionally withdrawn. You enjoy stability and don't embrace change.

2. **OBSTACLES:** There is a fine line between standing your ground and being stubborn. Make sure you are resisting for the right reasons.

3. **ROOT:** You are busy preparing the foundations. Although this may seem tedious, keep focusing on the bigger picture.

4. **PAST:** A past event where you were dedicated, loyal or responsible. It could have been a time when you were in charge of something.

5. **CROWN:** Be cautious and realistic. Now is not the time for new ideas. Stick with what you know works.

6. **NEAR FUTURE:** A period of rewarding hard work lies ahead. You are well-prepared to get the job done. A possible journey.

7. **FEAR:** You fear that all your hard work will be in vain.

8. **JUDGEMENT:** People see you as a trustworthy, stable and practical person. You are considered a good partner and friend.

9. **HOPE:** Desperately hoping that you will achieve your goals. You hope for material gain and financial stability.

10. **OUTCOME:** A structured and methodical time lies ahead. Work hard, remain focused and stick to your plans. Success will follow.

As a person, the Knight of Pentacles is stable, reliable and ambitious. He can be conservative, stubborn and not show his emotions. He works hard to provide for the people he loves. He may be an Earth sign (Taurus, Virgo or Capricorn).

OPPOSING CARDS

 **EIGHT OF WANDS**
rushing ahead

REINFORCING CARDS

 **THE EMPEROR**
dependable, practical

COURT CARD PAIRS

KNIGHT OF PENTACLES
(hard working)

KING OF CUPS
(idealistic)

Knight of Pentacles
- teaches the King to focus on the task at hand
- annoys the King when he pushes people too hard

• MATURE • PATIENT • KIND • LOYAL • GENEROUS • HARD WORKING • PROSPEROUS

Queen of Pentacles

This generous, patient, sensual woman could be you or someone else. She is kind, responsible and practical. The Queen of Pentacles works hard to get ahead and uses her talents. When she appears, this is a good time to follow a project through, invest in a home or consider marriage.

OVERVIEW
The Queen of Pentacles represents a practical and generous person who is financially independent and works hard but rests when time allows. This card advises you to approach issues in a sensible manner if you wish to be successful. Hard work will be required to reach your goal.

LOVE
If you are in a relationship, this card indicates that it is secure and that both partners are loyal. If representing a person, they are confident, generous, practical, nurturing and family orientated. If you are single, the Queen of Pentacles indicates that you should be selective when choosing a partner.

CAREER
You can achieve your goal if you are willing to put in the work, whether in terms of studying or advancing your career or business. Trust your instincts, but let common sense guide you.

SPIRITUALITY
Trust your instincts, meditate and spend time in nature to improve your intuition.

ADVICE
Many people may depend on you for advice. Be careful with your time and energy so that you do not end up depleted. Take time for yourself. Also, look at your finances – perhaps it is time to be cautious with expenditure.

DESCRIPTION
The Queen sits on a stone throne, staring at a coin, a symbol of wealth. The throne is carved with an angel (representing high status and purity), a goat (fertility and agility) and fruit (fertility and immortality). She is surrounded by a beautiful garden that represents nature, abundance, and the Earth. A rabbit in the foreground symbolises thoughtfulness, intelligence and luck. The mountains in the background show the challenges she has overcome.

• SUCCESSFUL • FINANCIALLY INDEPENDENT • LUXURY • ORGANISED

Celtic Cross Positions

1. **SIGNIFICATOR:** You are a financially successful, dependable and loyal person. You hold traditional family values in high regard.

2. **OBSTACLES:** You might be giving too much attention in one direction, either to your work or helping others. Finding balance is recommended.

3. **ROOT:** If you are considering settling down, now is a good time.

4. **PAST:** Something wonderful has ended, and you regret its passing. It can also indicate a recent form of stability in your life (either caused by a person or financial success).

5. **CROWN:** Efforts, hard work and practical planning are rewarded. There is an opportunity for growth and movement if you spend your money wisely and trust your instincts.

6. **NEAR FUTURE:** Growth of relationships and financial security. If you need practical help, perhaps there is a feminine influence you can go to for advice. Have faith in your abilities; now is the time for dreams to become reality.

7. **FEAR:** You have stopped believing in yourself and fear that you'll never amount to anything.

8. **JUDGEMENT:** An older woman who has a very comfortable life and can be counted on to give support. She is well-balanced and generous.

9. **HOPE:** You desire to be financially stable and able to help others.

10. **OUTCOME:** You'll achieve everything you want if you are willing to put in the work. Complete your current project by staying focused and grounded, and success will come your way. A period of satisfaction, pleasure and contentment.

As a person, the Queen of Pentacles is a mature female or feminine person who is generous and financially secure. She appreciates the finer things and is good at business. People come to her for advice. She may be an Earth sign (Taurus, Virgo or Capricorn).

OPPOSING CARDS

 **EIGHT OF SWORDS** confusion, limitations, powerlessness

REINFORCING CARDS

 **SIX OF WANDS** success, acclaim, achievement

COURT CARD PAIRS

QUEEN OF PENTACLES (down to earth)   **KING OF WANDS** (show off)

The Queen of Pentacles
- teaches the King enjoy the simple things in life
- annoys the King when she rejects anything showy.

• WEALTHY • SUCCESSFUL • GOOD LEADER • SECURITY • DISCIPLINE • INFLEXIBILITY • HARD WORKING

King of Pentacles

As a person, the King of Pentacles represents someone who is responsible, dependable and mature. The King has excellent business and financial abilities. Status and social position are extremely important to him. If representing a situation, it can suggest financial success.

OVERVIEW
In general, the King of Pentacles is a charismatic person who is successful in everything they do. Although he lacks creativity, he is dependable and realistic. It can also indicate that your finances are about to improve and that you might achieve the status you desire.

LOVE
If you are in a relationship, this card implies that your partner is stable and loving. If representing a person, the King of Pentacles depicts a grounded, mature person who is patient, reliable and sensual. If you are single, this card suggests you desire a deep, meaningful relationship.

CAREER
A brilliant card to draw in a career reading. The King of Pentacles indicates that your finances are about to improve. Hard work, integrity and common sense will be required to achieve your goals. You may receive advice from an older, successful person.

SPIRITUALITY
Now that you have achieved financial prosperity, you have the energy and time to pursue spirituality and find a deeper meaning to life.

ADVICE
Enjoy what you have achieved, and don't allow others to make you feel guilty about your success. Don't become inflexible.

DESCRIPTION
The King sits on a throne with carvings of bulls decorating it. The bulls represent Taurus (symbolising loyalty and stubbornness). He looks down at the pentacle on his lap, symbolising his wealth. The sceptre he holds indicates his power and authority. His clock is decorated with grape vines (showing harvest, pleasure and fertility). His left foot rests on a stone, representing a boar's head (strength and courage).

• STATUS • DEPENDABLE • RESPONSIBLE • FAITHFULNESS • INTEGRITY • STABILITY

Celtic Cross Positions

1 SIGNIFICATOR: You are charismatic and successful but can be jealous and possessive if threatened.

2 OBSTACLES: Turn your dreams into practical action by assessing your skills and being realistic. Be cautious of becoming arrogant.

3 ROOT: Either you are being over-cautious and holding yourself back. Or you are obsessed with finances to the exclusion of all else.

4 PAST: A stable person of integrity in your past whose advice had lingering effects on the current situation. Someone who carried the burden of responsibility.

5 CROWN: You are possibly moving into a period of stability. It may also suggest that a hard-working, responsible person is involved in the situation or can be turned to for advice.

6 NEAR FUTURE: Suggests that a financially secure future is possible if you embrace the qualities of the King. Stable, cautious behaviour is recommended at this time. A possible marriage or family commitment.

7 FEAR: You fear financial insecurity or business failure.

8 JUDGEMENT: People consider you to be an enterprising person who finds opportunity everywhere and succeeds at whatever you set your mind to.

9 HOPE: A desire to be looked at with respect and admiration. A desire to be successful and have it all – financial and material success, a happy marriage, and a satisfying home life.

10 OUTCOME: You are likely to reach your potential if you continue along your current path. You will be rewarded if you work hard, keep your focus steady and take it step by step. If you have a plan in mind, get started. It is destined for success.

As a person, the King of Pentacles is mature, patient, successful, generous and hard working. He does not take unnecessary risks. He is stubborn but faithful and values social acceptance. He may be an Earth sign (Taurus, Virgo or Capricorn).

OPPOSING CARDS

 **THE DEVIL**
impulsive, selfish

REINFORCING CARDS

 **THE EMPEROR**
stable, dependable, good leadership

COURT CARD PAIRS

KING OF PENTACLES (calm) **KNIGHT OF CUPS** (exciting)

King of Pentacles
- teaches the Knight how to be calm under pressure
- annoys the Knight because he is so predictable

The Suit of Swords

The Suit of Swords is focused on the intellect, rational thought and logic. This suit symbolises the delicate balance between power and intelligence.

If there are many Swords in a reading, you are likely dealing with mental struggles, arguments and decisions.

The negative side of Swords includes being ruthless, domineering, confrontational and rigid.

Element: Air

Keywords: intelligent, confrontational, ruthless, power, stress, difficulties

Corresponding playing card suit: Spades

Astrological signs: Aquarius, Gemini or Libra

Noted for: intellect and mentality

Ace of Swords

new ideas, clarity

Two of Swords

crossroads, stalemate

Three of Swords
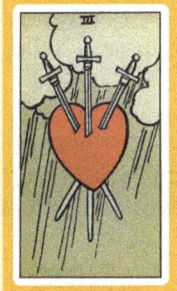
heartache, brutal insight

Four of Swords

rest, retreat, recuperate

Five of Swords

loss, betrayal, humiliation

Six of Swords

departure, movement

Seven of Swords

deception, theft

Eight of Swords

indecision, trapped

Nine of Swords

despair, suffering

Ten of Swords

failure, desperation

Page of Swords

messages, inspiration

Knight of Swords

decisive, confrontational

Queen of Swords

self-sufficient, confident

King of Swords

assertive, intimidating

• NEW IDEAS • INTELLECTUAL • CLARITY • LOGICAL • POTENTIAL • UNCOMPROMISING

Ace of Swords

DESCRIPTION
A hand in the clouds holds an upright sword. The hand is that of the Divine, reminding us that the energy of the Ace comes from above. The laurel around the sword represents victory and peace. The six petals symbolise luck. In the background, the jagged mountains remind us that there are still challenges to overcome.

The Ace of Swords suggests a new beginning and the ability to see things clearly. A flash of clarity that allows you to understand the situation and make a decision, remove what is no longer relevant and plan your future.

OVERVIEW
In a general context, the Ace of Swords represents new projects, beginnings and breakthroughs. It suggests that change is on the horizon, but first you need to make a choice. This decision needs to be unemotional, using only cool, clear intellect and rational thought.

LOVE
If there are difficulties in your relationship, you may need to solve them by using a logical approach rather than an emotional one. If you are single, the Ace of Swords suggests you might meet a new partner with whom you can share an intellectual connection.

CAREER
An auspicious card to draw in a career spread. Represents new projects, ideas and ventures. Consider applying for a new job that tests your boundaries. If a decision needs to be made, do so using logic and facts rather than emotion or intuition.

SPIRITUALITY
A moment of clarity may cause you to question your belief system and set you on a new path.

ADVICE
You need to admit to your successes and failures and be honest about your strengths and weaknesses. We can only truly be successful if we are honest with ourselves about our capabilities.

• DECISION • TRUTH • VISION • ACHIEVEMENT • FOCUS

Celtic Cross Positions

1. **SIGNIFICATOR:** You are a logical, successful person. You make decisions based on fact, not emotion, and therefore you can be perceived as aloof.

2. **OBSTACLES:** Your heart and mind are at odds with each other. You are encouraged to listen to your logical side at present.

3. **ROOT:** Something needs to end in order for new things to begin.

4. **PAST:** A previous decision led to failure and still holds you back. Make peace with the situation and forgive yourself.

5. **CROWN:** A decision needs to be made. Trust your inner resources to help you make the best choice.

6. **NEAR FUTURE:** Be ready for the opportunities coming. Use your intellect to make choices. New possibilities for success. Also indicates the moment of clarity and the ending of something.

7. **FEAR:** You fear being out of control or being too emotional.

8. **JUDGEMENT:** Represents a clear-headed, intellectual and honest person who is emotionally distant.

9. **HOPE:** You hope for clarity and want to see the truth.

10. **OUTCOME:** Clarity leads to good decisions and success. Think and analyse the situation from all angles before making a choice. Don't let your emotions cloud your judgment.

OPPOSING CARDS

THE MOON
unclear, illogical, hidden danger

FOUR OF CUPS
unmotivated, withdrawal

REINFORCING CARDS

WHEEL OF FORTUNE
change of fortune, opportunities

TWO OF WANDS
potential, discovery

REINFORCING CARDS

An Ace-Ace pair shows that a new spirit is entering your life. It draws on the energy of the Ace of Swords (intelligence, reason, justice, truth, clarity), plus one of these:

ACE OF CUPS
deep feelings, intimacy, compassion, love

ACE OF PENTACLES
prosperity, abundance, trust, grounded

ACE OF WANDS
creativity, excitement, adventure, courage

1. Beginning

• STALEMATE • DENIAL • CROSSROADS • BLOCKED FEELINGS • DIVIDED LOYALTY

Two of Swords

The Two of Swords represents being unable to choose a way forward. Being stuck in the process of weighing up options but unable to see clearly or unwilling to accept the truth.

OVERVIEW
You are possibly in a negative situation because you are either unwilling or incapable of accepting what is happening. You might be repressing your feelings or denying the truth. You could also be caught in an argument between others and have divided loyalties. You need to face the situation and do something about it.

LOVE
In a relationship, the Two of Swords suggests that you might be experiencing stalemate or an unwillingness to face issues. If single, you could have a choice to make. You might also be battling with being honest because expressing your feelings makes you feel vulnerable.

CAREER
In a career reading, this card can indicate you feel caught in the middle of a work conflict. You might also be facing a difficult choice between two career options.

SPIRITUALITY
In a spiritual reading, this card suggests that you are seeking balance in your spiritual life. Meditation may bring clarity.

ADVICE
You are hiding behind walls and refuse to open yourself up to others. Perhaps you feel that if you don't become emotionally attached, you will avoid conflict. This card suggests that many beautiful opportunities await if you open up and accept the help of others.

DESCRIPTION
A woman sits on a chair on a beach. She is blindfolded and cannot see her situation clearly. She holds two swords in balance, suggesting she is considering both options equally. The arms across her heart imply that she does not allow emotions into the situation. The rocks indicate that difficulties lie ahead. This situation is her choice; she is not a victim. She can stand up and walk away at any point. The new moon suggests new beginnings.

• PAINFUL CHOICES • PROCRASTINATION • CAUGHT IN THE MIDDLE • DECISIONS

Celtic Cross Positions

1. **SIGNIFICATOR:** You feel weighed down by a heavy decision. You might be in denial and refusing to accept the truth of the situation.

2. **OBSTACLES:** You may feel torn and unable to choose. Diplomacy and logic might be required to figure out the best way forward. Alternatively, look within yourself – perhaps you intuitively know the correct answer.

3. **ROOT:** Represents an unwillingness to accept the truth. But deep down, you know that you can only move forward if you take responsibility.

4. **PAST:** Represents a period when you were stuck in a situation and unwilling or incapable of making a choice. This may still be affecting you.

5. **CROWN:** A difficult choice has been made. You need to stay committed to your decision.

6. **NEAR FUTURE:** A situation of stalemate. A choice will need to be made. Once you see the truth of the issue, you might realise that things are not as bad as they seem.

7. **FEAR:** You fear facing the truth and feeling vulnerable.

8. **JUDGEMENT:** People see you as someone with divided loyalties or unable to make a choice.

9. **HOPE:** You hope the decision will become unnecessary if you wait long enough.

10. **OUTCOME:** Represents a dispute or unpleasant situation. Things will change as soon as you accept the truth. A possible argument. A choice needs to be made.

OPPOSING CARDS

THE FOOL
opening up, uninhibited

WHEEL OF FORTUNE
moving, getting things going

JUSTICE
accepting the truth, taking responsibility

THE STAR
free flow of positive feelings

THREE OF WANDS
moving forward, looking at the facts

REINFORCING CARDS

THE MOON
self-deception, not seeing the truth

NINE OF WANDS
being defensive, closing yourself off

SEVEN OF SWORDS
running away from the truth

FOUR OF PENTACLES
stalemate, blockage

2 Duality, balance, harmony, reflection

• PAIN • CONFLICT • SORROW • GRIEF • DISAPPOINTMENT • BRUTAL INSIGHT

Three of Swords

The Three of Swords represents a time of loss, heartache and suffering. It is one of the most difficult cards in the Tarot deck. The only silver lining offered is that suffering can help us grow.

OVERVIEW
When you see this card, expect sadness on your horizon. It indicates a period of difficulty, loss and betrayal. It may affect you directly or someone close to you.

LOVE
The Three of Swords is not a pleasant card to draw if you are in a relationship. It indicates separation, betrayal and divorce. If you are single, now is not a good time to consider a new relationship.

CAREER
In a career spread, this card can represent the loss of your job, increasing stress or feeling unhappy in the workplace. Arguments, deceit or unexpected losses are all possible.

SPIRITUALITY
Indicates you may be consumed with negative feelings about yourself. In order to heal, you need to forgive yourself and take time to rest.

ADVICE
Are you jealous of your partner without reason? Do you fear rejection or loneliness? A relationship can only survive if there is trust.

DESCRIPTION
A red heart is pierced by three swords. Raindrops fall from storm clouds. Pain, heartache and sorrow radiate from this card. But the storm won't last forever. We must be content with the knowledge that this, too, shall pass.

• HEARTBREAK • HURT • DISILLUSIONMENT • CONFLICT • SUFFERING

Celtic Cross Positions

1. **SIGNIFICATOR:** You are suffering on a deep level. There may be old hurts that have not fully healed, or you are experiencing a new trauma.

2. **OBSTACLES:** You need to face the truth of the situation and accept the part you played in this.

3. **ROOT:** Dishonesty or inner conflict lies at the heart of this situation. Honesty is the best way forward.

4. **PAST:** Heartache or an intense period of depression in your past affects the current situation. Perhaps you have not fully healed, or the person who caused the pain is trying to get back into your life.

5. **CROWN:** A warning that there is something wrong. Perhaps things are happening behind your back. Trust your intuition, but examine the facts before jumping to conclusions.

6. **NEAR FUTURE:** Expect unhappiness or sorrow caused by a separation, loss or betrayal. A possible affair or another secret may come to light.

7. **FEAR:** You fear heartbreak, rejection, separation and loss.

8. **JUDGEMENT:** Someone who is hurting deeply or whose selfishness has led to trauma and heartache.

9. **HOPE:** You hope for honesty and trust.

10. **OUTCOME:** A dreadful or disappointing discovery which turns your world upside down. Betrayal, abandonment, rejection, separation or pain. A difficult time lies ahead.

OPPOSING CARDS

THE LOVERS
intimacy, feeling love

THREE OF CUPS
companionship, trust

TEN OF CUPS
joy, love, peace, togetherness

REINFORCING CARDS

FIVE OF CUPS
separation, heartache, loss of love

NINE OF SWORDS
anguish, heartbreak

FIVE OF PENTACLES
rejection, separation, lack of support

3 Trio, planning, ideas, creation

REST • RETREAT • TIME OUT • MEDITATION • RECUPERATION • PREPARATION

Four of Swords

The Four of Swords suggests rest and withdrawal. This often follows a period of high stress, heavy workloads or conflict. It tells you to slow down, take time out and replenish.

OVERVIEW
After periods of intense stress, we often can't think straight. We may feel emotionally exhausted, depressed or overwhelmed. The Four of Swords tells us that now is the time to rest and recharge. It can also suggest taking a step back from a recent argument. Perhaps both sides need time to reflect before a resolution is possible.

LOVE
If you are in a relationship, the Four of Swords suggests that you and your partner will benefit from some time apart. If you are single, this is not the time to start a new relationship. You need to heal yourself first.

CAREER
In a career reading, this card can indicate that you've been under immense work pressure and feeling overwhelmed. You need to take a break before beginning your next project.

SPIRITUALITY
As you withdraw from activity, this is a good time to focus on meditation and your spiritual side.

ADVICE
This card advises you to rest when you are tired. Rest doesn't imply being lazy – you can use this time to plot and plan your next phase.

DESCRIPTION
A knight lies on top of a tomb in a church in full armour. His hands are in the prayer position. He looks at peace. Three swords hang above him, and one lies below. The woman and child in the stained glass window indicate that he can rejoin the outside world when he is ready. But for now, the church is a place of sanctuary, a safe place to rest.

4 Stability, order, making things happen

• TAKING STOCK • SLOWING DOWN • CONTEMPLATION

Celtic Cross Positions

1. **SIGNIFICATOR:** You feel emotionally exhausted after a stressful period and are unable to think clearly.

2. **OBSTACLES:** Withdrawal, recuperation, meditation. Represents the need to take time out. You may feel you cannot afford this time off, but the cost will be much higher if you don't take it.

3. **ROOT:** Don't make decisions while you are feeling exhausted. You need to slow down and withdraw. This is not a defeat; just a quiet moment between the end of a stage and the beginning of another.

4. **PAST:** A recent time of withdrawal or conflict is affecting the current situation. You may have gone through a period of intense stress and are still recovering. An unresolved argument might still be hanging over you and affecting your mental well-being.

5. **CROWN:** Clarity can only be gained by stepping back from the situation and thinking about it objectively.

6. **NEAR FUTURE:** Represents the need to rest after a stressful time. You might have reached the end of your physical, mental or emotional resources. Allowing yourself to rest will give you a different perspective.

7. **FEAR:** You fear being alone or making the wrong choice. You may be worried about the financial, relationship, family or career implications of taking time off.

8. **JUDGEMENT:** A person who is withdrawn or suffering burnout.

9. **HOPE:** You desire to be back on track. Exhaustion can take a long time to heal, and waiting to feel normal again can be frustrating.

10. **OUTCOME:** Represents the pause between phases. Although a new phase is about to begin, you need to take a moment to recuperate, regroup and plan your next move. Can also imply a well-deserved holiday or rest.

OPPOSING CARDS

THE MAGICIAN
being active, focusing outward

WHEEL OF FORTUNE
rapid pace, lots of movement

EIGHT OF WANDS
making your move, rushing

TEN OF WANDS
overexerting, taking on too much

TWO OF PENTACLES
having fun, balancing many activities

REINFORCING CARDS

THE HIGH PRIESTESS
resting quietly, contemplating

THE HERMIT
contemplating, being quiet

HANGED MAN
rest, suspended activity

FOUR OF CUPS
contemplating, taking time alone

SIX OF SWORDS
rest, recovery

• DEFEAT • HUMILIATION • SPITE • LOSS • LIMITATIONS • EMPTY VICTORY • CONFLICT

Five of Swords

The Five of Swords is a card of conflict showing either your defeat or your victory. Neither is easy, as the defeat highlights your limitations, and the victory is hollow because underhand tactics were used.

DESCRIPTION
A battle has been fought. Two defeated opponents walk away, their stance conveying a feeling of sadness and loss. The victor watches them with an unpleasant expression on his face. He holds three swords, with two more lying nearby. The jagged clouds hint that the battle is not yet over. There is a feeling that the victor used underhand tactics to win the battle. His smirk suggests that he feels no remorse.

OVERVIEW
In a general context, the Five of Swords can represent defeat, surrender or walking away. You might be leaving a toxic environment (such as harassment or bullying) or have lost an argument and need to accept defeat. It can also imply that you've got your way by being deceitful or dishonest.

LOVE
This card is not a good omen if you are in a relationship. It suggests separation and divorce. A third party might be the cause of the conflict. If you are single, you may still be recovering from a past relationship that was unpleasant or controlling.

CAREER
The Five of Swords suggests stress, conflict and hostility in the workplace. Either you or a colleague are being dishonest and underhanded. Question your own motives and actions, and do your best to act with integrity and honesty.

SPIRITUALITY
This card suggests someone is trying to control your spiritual practice. Pay attention to what people say and question their motives.

ADVICE
When this card appears, question the motives of everyone in the situation, including your own. You may desire to win but is the price worth it?

• HARASSMENT • COMPETITION • CONQUEST • THREAT • CONFLICTING INTERESTS

Celtic Cross Positions

1 SIGNIFICATOR: You have done something underhand or deceitful that you regret and feel ashamed about.

2 OBSTACLES: Hidden agendas and emotions are running high and make it difficult to understand the situation. It is time to put your needs first but do so with honour and integrity. A cheap victory has no real value.

3 ROOT: Hostility lies at the heart of this situation. Either you or someone else is being arrogant or controlling.

4 PAST: A time of conflict and poor communication. Lack of compassion caused unnecessary pain.

5 CROWN: Inner conflict prevents you from seeing the situation clearly. You might have difficulty moving on. You need to make peace and forgive yourself.

6 NEAR FUTURE: Things are not going to plan, and you might be considering dishonest behaviour in order to salvage the situation. Alternatively, you might soon be the victim of dishonesty.

7 FEAR: You fear confrontation or someone discovering your dishonesty.

8 JUDGEMENT: A selfish person who has little regard for others. Someone who considers winning more important than honour.

9 HOPE: You hope for an easy victory.

10 OUTCOME: You will find yourself in a situation that you desperately want to win. Examine your motives and try to see things from your opponent's perspective. Hostility and dishonesty. You may be the victim or the perpetrator of malicious gossip, humiliation or abuse.

OPPOSING CARDS

THE EMPEROR
following the rules, obeying the law

JUSTICE
having integrity, doing what is right

TEMPERANCE
working with others, harmony, cooperation

SIX OF CUPS
innocent, kind, well-intentioned

REINFORCING CARDS

WHEEL OF FORTUNE
a change in fortune

FIVE OF WANDS
discord, people set against each other

SEVEN OF WANDS
me against them mentality, conflict

SEVEN OF SWORDS
dishonour, separation from others

5 Adaptation, challenge, conflict

• CHANGE • MOVEMENT • NEW PERSPECTIVE • RECOVERY • LIBERATION

Six of Swords

The Six of Swords suggests that you are at a crossroads but that the worst is over, and you will be leaving current difficulties behind. Can represent a physical, mental or spiritual journey. It may indicate moving house.

DESCRIPTION

A woman and child are huddled in a boat. A man rows them to land on the other side. The water is choppy on one side of the boat, but the sea ahead is calm, suggesting that her troubles are almost over. The six swords in the boat indicate that although she has left her life behind, she still carries burdens with her. Her figure is hunched and covered, suggesting sadness or loss. This isn't an easy journey.

OVERVIEW
The Six of Swords represents a conscious decision to leave something behind, perhaps to escape a difficult situation. You are moving into calmer waters. It might also represent the need for a holiday after a particularly stressful time. You could also be running away from your troubles.

LOVE
If you are in a relationship, you've likely overcome a difficult moment. If you are currently having problems, this card advises that you spend time getting to know your partner on a deeper level. If you are single, it suggests a period of stillness and healing before entering a new relationship.

CAREER
In a career reading, the Six of Swords indicates a period of calm after an extremely busy time. Can also suggest that you need to consider if your career choice brings you happiness. Travel, transfer or moving to a new position are also possibilities.

SPIRITUALITY
In a spiritual context, the Six of Swords suggests a transition. Can also indicate inner travel and spirit walking.

ADVICE
The decision to leave everything behind can seem petrifying at first. But believe in yourself. Sometimes this is necessary for growth and to allow new things to enter your life.

• DEPARTURE • TRANSITION • NEW COURSE • SOLUTION • LIGHT AT END OF TUNNEL

Celtic Cross Positions

1. **SIGNIFICATOR:** You have made the difficult decision to leave your current situation. You are worried about the future.

2. **OBSTACLES:** You are considering changing the direction of your life. Examine your motives to make sure you aren't running away.

3. **ROOT:** Difficulties. Feeling unable to escape and trapped in your life. You cannot see a clear way forward.

4. **PAST:** You recently made a decision to leave a situation behind. You are still adapting to your new life and carry an emotional burden.

5. **CROWN:** The weight of decisions that need to be made hangs heavy on your shoulders. You may feel apathetic, lost and depressed. You need to accept where you are and what you've done, and work with what you have.

6. **NEAR FUTURE:** You may currently feel trapped either by stress or responsibilities. Trust that you have the resolve to overcome your problems. The storm will pass. It can also suggest travel.

7. **FEAR:** You fear the unknown and letting go.

8. **JUDGEMENT:** Someone who leaves when things get difficult or someone who is carrying a heavy burden.

9. **HOPE:** Represents hope for peace and a life without conflict. Hope for new beginnings and a second chance.

10. **OUTCOME:** New beginnings. You have chosen to leave your old life behind and are now heading into the unknown. You may not yet see the way forward, but you need to trust that you are headed towards better times. We must sometimes walk away from certain things to make space for new adventures and to live our true lives. Can also suggest travel for work or pleasure.

OPPOSING CARDS

STRENGTH
having heart, unshakable resolve

THE SUN
vitality, enthusiasm

FOUR OF WANDS
excitement, celebration

THREE OF CUPS
high spirits, exuberance

REINFORCING CARDS

TEN OF WANDS
getting by, struggling along

FOUR OF CUPS
feeling listless, depressed, uncaring

FIVE OF CUPS
sadness

EIGHT OF CUPS
moving on, going on a trip

FOUR OF SWORDS
rest, recovery

6 Patterns, togetherness

• DECEPTION • CHEATING • STEALING • DISHONESTY • TRICKS • SUBTERFUGE

Seven of Swords

The Seven of Swords represents deception, theft and dishonesty. Either it symbolises you or someone in your life. A time to tread cautiously.

OVERVIEW
In a general context, the Seven of Swords can recommend that you do not disclose all information. Dishonesty surrounds you, so it's best to play things safe. However, it can also indicate that you are the cause of the dishonesty. This card encourages caution and warns you against blind trust.

LOVE
If you are in a relationship, this card hints at deception, lies and betrayal. If you are single, be cautious of new people as deceit is indicated.

CAREER
This card indicates that there might be trickery or deceit in the workplace. Protect yourself against possible sabotage. Someone might be plotting against you. Also suggests that you are not being honest in your dealings with others.

SPIRITUALITY
This card advises you not to trust anyone at face value. Question everything and everyone. Let your intuition guide you when making decisions.

ADVICE
A difficult time as you are not sure who you can trust. Or perhaps you feel forced to act in an underhand manner. Question your motives and make sure that you will be able to live with yourself afterwards.

DESCRIPTION
A man sneaks away from a military camp carrying five swords. His behaviour indicates that he has stolen them. Two swords remain behind, suggesting that the situation isn't over. The thief acts alone and seems proud of his deceit.

• CUNNING • EVASIVE • STEALTHY • AVOIDING RESPONSIBILITY

Celtic Cross Positions

1 SIGNIFICATOR: You have acted in a dishonest way, perhaps believing that the ends justify the means. Or you have been the victim of dishonesty.

2 OBSTACLES: Now is the time to act alone and rely on yourself. You are being watched and need to keep your actions honest.

3 ROOT: You are facing a challenge and can only triumph by acting unconventionally. Bold doesn't mean manipulative, so plan carefully.

4 PAST: Represents a choice that was made, possibly one you are no longer proud of. It could also refer to a time when somebody acted dishonestly behind your back.

5 CROWN: You are possibly avoiding the truth of the situation or avoiding your obligations. Take a step back and see things as they are.

6 NEAR FUTURE: Dishonest people surround you. Be careful who you trust. Or a situation has arisen, and you need to be economical with the truth. You may have been asked to keep a secret. Make sure that you aren't deceiving yourself or being manipulative.

7 FEAR: You fear being cheated or betrayed. You worry that your dishonest behaviour will be exposed.

8 JUDGEMENT: Represents someone sneaky and untrustworthy. Possibly a thief, not only of material items but also ideas, time or friendships.

9 HOPE: A desire to be bold and daring. To stand out and take risks.

10 OUTCOME: A situation may arise where you will have to act dishonestly in order to come out on top. Consider who will get hurt and examine other options before making your choice. Be careful – if you aren't being dishonest, someone might be plotting against you.

OPPOSING CARDS

THE HIEROPHANT
working within the group

JUSTICE
accepting responsibility, transparent

TEN OF WANDS
meeting obligations, being responsible

SIX OF CUPS
innocent, kind, open, noble

REINFORCING CARDS

THE HERMIT
being alone, staying away from others

TWO OF SWORDS
running from the truth

FIVE OF SWORDS
dishonour, separation from others

NINE OF PENTACLES
relying on yourself, acting on your own

7 Accomplishments, self-expansion

• INDECISION • PROCRASTINATION • ISOLATION • SELF-SABOTAGE • FEAR • RESTRICTION • VICTIMISATION

Eight of Swords

The Eight of Swords represents feeling trapped and not knowing how to move forward. Indecision and confusion keep you stuck in this position. Once you make a choice, a new path will open up.

OVERVIEW
The Eight of Swords suggests that you feel imprisoned or restricted. However, things may not be as bad as they seem. You could simply be paralysed by your own fears and negative thoughts. It also implies that you are trapped in a controlling relationship.

LOVE
If you are in a relationship, the Eight of Swords suggests you might have a dominating partner. You may need to make some difficult decisions in order to put yourself first. If you are single, now is not the right time to start a relationship. Focus on getting your life on track first.

CAREER
In a career reading, the Eight of Swords suggests that you feel stuck in a dead-end job or disillusioned by the hamster-wheel-cycle of work and life. You might feel powerless or confused about the way forward.

SPIRITUALITY
In a spiritual context, the Eight of Swords suggests that you feel restricted and powerless in choosing your path.

ADVICE
Focus, find clarity and give your future some thought. Once you know where you want to go, things often slot into place. Don't wait to be rescued. You need to take charge and figure this out for yourself.

DESCRIPTION
A woman is bound and blindfolded. She stands on boggy ground and is surrounded by eight swords. Although things seem bleak, her situation isn't that bad. She is not tightly bound and could free herself easily. There is a way out of the swords and she could find help in the nearby village. However, she cannot see these possibilities because her mind is clouded with doubt. The water at her feet suggests that she should allow her intuition to guide her.

• FEELING POWERLESS • LIMITATIONS • ABANDONMENT • CHANGE IN DIRECTION

Celtic Cross Positions

1 SIGNIFICATOR: You feel trapped by a situation and are unable to decide on the best way forward.

2 OBSTACLES: You cannot wait to be saved, you need to rescue yourself.

3 ROOT: You are lost, confused and powerless. You feel bound and trapped by the illusions you have created.

4 PAST: A recent co-dependant relationship or a time when you broke free from a situation that made you feel imprisoned.

5 CROWN: A state of confusion, vulnerability and hopelessness. Waiting for someone to save you.

6 NEAR FUTURE: You may feel trapped by an unpleasant situation, a controlling partner or a dead-end job. The situation might not be as bleak as it seems. A solution may present itself.

7 FEAR: You fear being trapped or overlooked.

8 JUDGEMENT: Someone trapped in a negative situation and unable to see the available options.

9 HOPE: You desire to be free and have no restrictions. You want to feel like you have options.

10 OUTCOME: Represents feeling trapped and isolated. However, you may find solutions by using your intellect and making different choices, which can lead you in a new direction. There is a way out; all you need to do is find it.

OPPOSING CARDS

THE MAGICIAN
feeling powerful, aware of what's happening

THE CHARIOT
self-confidence, focus

TWO OF WANDS
power, boldness

FOUR OF WANDS
freedom, lack of restriction

THREE OF PENTACLES
competence, know-how, planning

REINFORCING CARDS

THE DEVIL
confusion, restriction

THE MOON
confusion, lack of clarity

TEN OF SWORDS
victim mentality, powerlessness

8 Inspiration, structure, balance

• DESPAIR • DEPRESSION • SUFFERING • ANXIETY • GUILT • WORRY • SORROW • LOSS • MISERY

Nine of Swords

DESCRIPTION
A woman sits up in bed during the night. She holds her face in her hands as though she is sobbing. The nine swords on the wall represent her negative thoughts. Her quilt is adorned with red roses and outlines of astrological symbols.

The Nine of Swords represents fear and grief. But it also shows the overwhelming power of negative thoughts. When we exaggerate thoughts of impending doom, it feels as though the world is about to end.

OVERVIEW
The Nine of Swords suggests that you may be worrying about something that has not yet happened – and may never happen – but thinking about its possibility leaves you paralysed with fear. Or perhaps you are dealing with something that has either left you hating yourself and feeling guilty or broken with sorrow. Feeling overwhelmed and unable to cope, you may have reached a breaking point. It can also signify feeling isolated or suffering from nightmares and insomnia.

LOVE
If you are in a relationship, the Nine of Swords suggests that it may be ending. You may been experiencing regret, remorse or guilt brought on by infidelity or deception. If you are single, a past relationship still weighs heavy on your mind. Perhaps you have yet to recover or to forgive yourself.

CAREER
The Nine of Swords suggests stress and unhappiness are causing anguish and anxiety at work. If you don't make a change, you may become overwhelmed.

SPIRITUALITY
This card suggests that you likely feel detached or isolated from your spiritual side.

ADVICE
Try to stop worrying about things that you can't control. For things you can change, stop looking at the big picture. Break it down into small achievable tasks.

• LAMENTATION • FEAR • NEGATIVITY • DEEP UNHAPPINESS • BURDENED • AT BREAKING POINT

Celtic Cross Positions

1. **SIGNIFICATOR:** You are consumed by anxiety and anguish. Pain makes you unable to see the way forward. You may be overly self-critical.

2. **OBSTACLES:** Guilt from past actions renders you incapable of making decisions and moving on.

3. **ROOT:** Represents a deep unhappiness caused by guilt, circumstance or grief. You feel your world is ending.

4. **PAST:** Represents a traumatic experience in your recent past from which you are still recovering. It has left you feeling vulnerable.

5. **CROWN:** Obsessive thoughts prevent you from thinking clearly and do not bring you closer to a resolution. Take positive steps to move forward.

6. **NEAR FUTURE:** Represents a time of deep unhappiness. You are at a breaking point. Life feels like it is crashing down around you.

7. **FEAR:** You fear being alone or losing someone close to you. A fear of things ending.

8. **JUDGEMENT:** Someone experiencing grief due to past hardship. Depression and loneliness.

9. **HOPE:** You are hoping for the pain to end.

10. **OUTCOME:** The path ahead might be difficult. You need to consider if you are making the right choice. A time of being alone with your worries. If prospects look bleak, let something go or make a small change.

OPPOSING CARDS

THE STAR
serenity, peace of mind

JUDGEMENT
lack of guilt, absolution

THREE OF CUPS
being on top of the world

SIX OF CUPS
innocence

TEN OF CUPS
joy, peace, delight

REINFORCING CARDS

THE DEVIL
despair, lack of joy

TEN OF WANDS
worrying

THREE OF SWORDS
anguish, heartbreak

SIX OF SWORDS
depression, sadness

9 Concepts come together

• BETRAYAL • RUIN • PAIN • FAILURE • BITTERNESS • ENEMIES • DARK BEFORE THE DAWN

Ten of Swords

The Ten of Swords represents failure, destruction and hopelessness. But, as with all tens, it symbolises the end of a cycle. After this, you'll rise from the ashes as a new cycle begins.

OVERVIEW
The Ten of Swords indicates an ending of something that was important to you, such as a relationship, a career, a home or a path. It can also signify betrayal and being stabbed in the back. A painful learning experience, but there is light on the horizon.

LOVE
If you are in a relationship, this card suggests that it may be coming to an end. It can also indicate betrayal and infidelity. If you are single, perhaps you are still feeling the effects of your last relationship.

CAREER
In a career Tarot reading, the Ten of Swords can indicate that your current role or business venture might be ending. Things have not worked out as you'd hoped, and it's time to think about a different direction, approach, or career.

SPIRITUALITY
This card indicates that you may have decided to abandon your previous belief system.

ADVICE
The quicker you learn from this experience, the sooner you'll be able to move on. Don't play the victim or the martyr. Accept where you are, heal and move on.

DESCRIPTION
A man lies face down, apparently dead, with ten swords in his back. A red cape is draped over him, offering a sign of dignity. The sky looks ominous, but the sun is rising, bringing hope and new opportunities. The calm sea suggests that even in times of darkness, peace and calm can be found.

• BACKSTABBING • BREAKDOWN • COLLAPSE • EXHAUSTION • INABILITY TO COPE

Celtic Cross Positions

1. **SIGNIFICATOR:** You feel defeated, and everything seems bleak. Hopelessness, ruin, exhaustion.

2. **OBSTACLES:** Letting go is the only way forward, although it may be painful. Look for a glimmer of light to show you a new direction or give you hope.

3. **ROOT:** Those who wish you ill may be plotting against you. Keep your eyes open and your friends close. Or you may be recovering from a painful experience.

4. **PAST:** A very trying past event where you hit rock bottom. It was a difficult lesson, but it helped you grow as a person.

5. **CROWN:** Don't play the victim and feel sorry for yourself. Accept your role in what has happened and take responsibility.

6. **NEAR FUTURE:** Something is about to end, and it will be painful. This is unavoidable as things are currently in motion. You likely already know what is coming and have a moment to prepare yourself.

7. **FEAR:** You fear loss, failure and misfortune.

8. **JUDGEMENT:** Someone who exaggerates, is attention-seeking and tends to be melodramatic. Or someone who has suffered a great deal.

9. **HOPE:** You hope for a speedy resolution and a better future.

10. **OUTCOME:** Represents a very difficult time ahead. Misfortune, pain and failure. This is either caused by a betrayal or by your own actions. This moment is likely to be short-lived and indicates that you've reached a turning point.

OPPOSING CARDS

THE CHARIOT
self-assertion, power, victory

THE SUN
happiness, contentment

TWO OF WANDS
power, self-confidence

SIX OF WANDS
self-promotion, being on top of the world

NINE OF CUPS
satisfaction, happy with conditions

REINFORCING CARDS

THE HANGED MAN
sacrifice, martyrdom

EIGHT OF SWORDS
victim mentality, powerlessness

10 Completion, success, transformation

• MESSAGES • SURPRISES • NEWS • DISCERNMENT • IDEAS • INSPIRATION • PLANNING

Page of Swords

The Page of Swords refers either to a situation or a person. If it is a situation, you can expect good news and new ideas. It can also suggest recklessness and an insatiable thirst for knowledge.
It advises you to examine the situation thoroughly before making a decision.

OVERVIEW
The Page of Swords is generally a positive card that brings news, ideas, and inspiration. However, it also speaks of conflicts and advises you to be patient and use your intellect. It can suggest the early stages of negotiation or an idea that will tantalise you.

LOVE
If you are in a relationship, arguments and conflict are indicated. If you are single, you'll need to be more outgoing if you want to meet someone.

CAREER
In a career reading, the Page of Swords suggests you are ambitious and full of ideas. This may threaten people who don't have the same level of intelligence and drive as you do. Can also indicate considering a course of study or a new business idea.

SPIRITUALITY
This card suggests that now is a good time to embrace more spiritual aspects after a period of focusing on mundane matters.

ADVICE
You may think you know it all and have all the answers, but this way of thinking leads to arrogance. Question yourself, challenge your beliefs and opinions, and listen to the wisdom of others.

DESCRIPTION
A young man holds a sword to the sky. His body and sword lean in the same direction, but he faces the opposite way. His stance shows that he is ready for action but patiently considers all aspects before making his move. A breeze indicates movement and energy.
The landscape is fertile, showing positive change. The mountains, representing obstacles are small – almost insignificant – suggesting that they can be easily overcome. The birds in the sky symbolise messages and movement.

• VIGILANCE • GUARDED • READY FOR ACTION • INQUISITIVE • QUICK WITTED • LOGICAL

Celtic Cross Positions

1. **SIGNIFICATOR:** You are open to new ideas and are ready to put your energy into something.

2. **OBSTACLES:** You may feel people are trying to suppress your excitement. Look for new information, but don't allow the opinions of others to change your path.

3. **ROOT:** The situation is filled with the spirit of discovery, learning and excitement.

4. **PAST:** A past situation where you were very focused. Your ambition might have unintentionally created rifts with friends or colleagues.

5. **CROWN:** You are ready to face new challenges. You may need to stand your ground and defend yourself.

6. **NEAR FUTURE:** Negotiations or conflict during which you need to be patient and open to fresh ideas.

7. **FEAR:** You are scared of delayed news or impending negotiations.

8. **JUDGEMENT:** Represents a quick-thinking, intelligent person. Brimming with ideas, but often misunderstood. Restless and always on the lookout for a new challenge.

9. **HOPE:** You hope to receive positive news or advice on how best to resolve the current situation.

10. **OUTCOME:** Unexpected news could shake the foundations of your life. New ideas and opportunities arise. Perhaps an endeavour that takes you in an unexpected direction. You may face challenges but you have the intellect and wisdom to overcome them. Advice and information may come from unexpected places.

As a person, the Page of Swords represents an intellectual younger person who is strong-willed with an analytical and logical mind. A deep thinker who can be insensitive. A loner. Can also be a bit of a gossip. They follow the rules. Might be an Air sign (Aquarius, Gemini or Libra).

OPPOSING CARDS

 **THE HERMIT** prudence, withdrawal

 **FOUR OF PENTACLES** resistance to change, stagnation

REINFORCING CARDS

 **THE FOOL** spontaneity, recklessness

 **ACE OF CUPS** good news, new beginnings

 **KNIGHT OF WANDS** impulsive, daring, movement

• CAPABLE • MOVEMENT • RADICAL CHANGE • INTELLIGENCE • DECISIVE • OPPORTUNITIES

Knight of Swords

When you see the Knight of Swords, expect sudden movement and change. Decisions are taken quickly under the influence of the Knight.

OVERVIEW
The Knight of Swords is a positive card that indicates significant changes are coming quickly. You may need to embrace a rapidly moving situation and take charge. There may be little time for careful analysis or weighing up options. Jump in and do it.

LOVE
If you are in a relationship, the Knight of Swords brings sudden, unexpected movement. If you are single, you might meet someone who shares qualities with the Knight.

CAREER
In a career reading, this card suggests that ambition and determination drive the situation. Expect positive movement in your career and finances. A promotion, funding for a new project. Be bold and go for it.

SPIRITUALITY
A big change is coming in your spiritual life. Things are coming together, and you can expect some excitement.

ADVICE
Not everyone's intellect and drive travel at the same speed as yours. Try to be patient with those on a different wavelength.

DESCRIPTION
A Knight in armour races across the landscape on a white horse. His sword is held high as if ready for battle, symbolising his dedication. The wind seems to be blowing against him, but this does not deter him. The white horse represents the intellectual energy that drives him. The butterflies on the horse's banner symbolise transformation.

• CHAOTIC EVENT • CONFRONTATION • SELF-ASSURED • SEIZE THE MOMENT • ENERGY

Celtic Cross Positions

1. **SIGNIFICATOR:** You are intelligent and quick-witted but prone to impatience.

2. **OBSTACLES:** You need to examine the motives behind your impulsiveness to act.

3. **ROOT:** Ideas are bubbling inside you. The energy of the Knight promises change, but don't be reckless.

4. **PAST:** A recent rapid change that has led you to this situation. A time when you were brave or reckless.

5. **CROWN:** You'll soon be offered a chance to change your life. The decisions you make will affect your future for years to come.

6. **NEAR FUTURE:** A big change is coming. Perhaps an incredible idea will set you off on a new path, a job promotion will take you to another city, or a lover might sweep you off your feet. An exciting time lies ahead.

7. **FEAR:** You fear stagnation and loss of ideas. You are petrified that things will stay the same forever.

8. **JUDGEMENT:** A dramatic, intelligent person who can be impulsive. Exciting to be around.

9. **HOPE:** You wish for something exciting to happen. A deep desire that your current plan works and brings you everything you've hoped for.

10. **OUTCOME:** Represents a big change. Good news. Exciting times lie ahead. Possibly travel and a radical lifestyle change. New projects and opportunities.

If representing a person, the Knight of Swords is successful, clever and quick-witted. He can be reckless and impatient as he gets bored quickly. He is exciting, and people are drawn to him. He may be an Air sign (Aquarius, Gemini or Libra).

OPPOSING CARDS

 **EIGHT OF PENTACLES**
steady, consistent

REINFORCING CARDS

 **EIGHT OF WANDS**
action, progress, excitement

COURT CARD PAIRS

KNIGHT OF SWORDS (blunt)   **KNIGHT OF PENTACLES** (exciting)

Knight of Swords
- teaches the Knight of Pentacles to embrace change
- annoys the Knight of Pentacles by being impatient

• MATURE • INDEPENDENT • CONFIDENT • INTELLIGENT • PERCEPTIVE • HONEST • PROTECTIVE

Queen of Swords

The Queen of Swords is a very principled person and might come across as stern and emotionless. She represents the importance of sometimes making decisions using only the head, not the heart. She has compassion but is objective.

OVERVIEW
In a general context, the Queen of Swords can represent a person who embodies the characteristics of the Queen. She is realistic and sceptical, taking nothing at face value. You may receive constructive criticism or be challenged to be open-minded. This card can also indicate that you are still processing sadness from a past event.

LOVE
If you are in a relationship, the Queen of Swords can indicate that you need some distance from your partner. It can also represent someone who misses the freedom of being single. If you are not involved, the Queen suggests that you may meet someone with her qualities.

CAREER
In a career reading, this is a good communication card. You may do well in exams or tests. Someone in the workplace might offer assistance or advice.

SPIRITUALITY
This card indicates being logical may hinder your spiritual development.

ADVICE
Are you a perfectionist? Do you find fault with everyone and feel they cannot meet your expectations? If you don't want to end up alone and isolated, you might need to make your expectations more realistic.

DESCRIPTION
The Queen sits on a stone throne carved with cherubs (symbolising innocence) and butterflies (transformation), representing her gentler attributes. She faces the future, one hand holding a sword and the other beckoning. Butterflies adorn her crown, and her cloak is decorated with clouds. The sword suggests her commitment to the truth. The clouds are low but the sky above is clear, indicating that her troubles are almost over. A single bird flies.

• COMMUNICATIVE • PRACTICAL • SELF-SUFFICIENT • PRINCIPLED • REALISTIC

Celtic Cross Positions

1. **SIGNIFICATOR:** You are strong-willed, intelligent and do not let emotions take over.
2. **OBSTACLES:** Believe in yourself and trust your inner wisdom to work out a solution.
3. **ROOT:** Your strong principles are the cause of this situation. Try to be compassionate and understand where others are coming from.
4. **PAST:** You have recently been hurt and are still affected by this loss. To move on, you need to stop looking at the situation from an emotional perspective.
5. **CROWN:** Make sure your dreams aren't interfering with your responsibilities.
6. **NEAR FUTURE:** This situation calls for objectivity. Don't let your emotions get in the way. Rely on your intellect to get you through. A strong feminine influence in your life can be relied upon for advice in this situation.
7. **FEAR:** You fear being dependent or giving in to your emotions.
8. **JUDGEMENT:** Represents a strong, independent person who is emotionally unavailable.
9. **HOPE:** You hope for clarity and inner strength to overcome difficulties.
10. **OUTCOME:** Logical choices will help you create a better future for yourself. You might also be influenced by someone with the Queen's characteristics. If a past hurt still lingers, there is hope for recovery.

As a person, the Queen of Swords is chatty, independent and capable. Her past suffering has led to inner strength and wisdom. She will help those who cannot defend themselves. She may be an Air sign (Aquarius, Gemini or Libra).

OPPOSING CARDS

 **THE HIGH PRIESTESS**
intuition, hidden emotions

REINFORCING CARDS

 **NINE OF PENTACLES**
independent, confident

COURT CARD PAIRS

QUEEN OF SWORDS (honest)   **KNIGHT OF WANDS** (deceitful)

Queen of Swords
- teaches the Knight to be truthful
- annoys the Knight of Wands by seeing through his charm

• ARTICULATE • INTELLIGENT • AMBITIOUS • ASSERTIVE • CONFIDENT • INDEPENDENT • RESPECTED

King of Swords

The King of Swords can represent a person in your life with authority and power who is important at the time of this reading. This card also represents decisions, maturity, mastering your emotions and logical reasoning.

DESCRIPTION

A King sits on a throne, facing forwards. He wears blue, symbolising spiritual knowledge. His purple cape speaks of his compassion and intellect. The King holds a raised sword in his right hand (the hand of the rational mind). He sits in judgment, holding the power of truth and justice. His crown is decorated with cherubs and butterflies. Carved into his throne is a waxing and waning crescent moon.

OVERVIEW
In a general context, the King of Swords represents structure, authority, self-discipline and intelligence. This card advises that you use your intelligence to get through the current situation and not be too emotional. It can also suggest impending legal matters.

LOVE
If you are in a relationship, the King of Swords is generally a good sign. It indicates that your relationship might be heading to a new level of maturity. If you are single, you might meet someone with the qualities of the King.

CAREER
In a career reading, this card can represent an older person in the work environment who will challenge you in a positive way. Consider it a healthy learning experience. Watch out for getting involved in unnecessary arguments or getting too emotional at work.

SPIRITUALITY
Spiritually, this card suggests that your approach needs a bit more structure.

ADVICE
Are you too assertive? Have you blocked your emotional needs? Are you too quick to point out other people's mistakes? Others may find you domineering, and you risk ostracising yourself. Use your intellect to find balance.

• POWERFUL • INTIMIDATING. • MENTAL CLARITY • JUST • ANALYTICAL

Celtic Cross Positions

1. **SIGNIFICATOR:** You are a person of action, filled with ideas.

2. **OBSTACLES:** You might be in a position where you need to stand your ground and defend yourself.

3. **ROOT:** Don't let imposter syndrome affect you. You've reached a level of achievement and have mastered your trade. You are capable and deserving. If you believe in yourself, you can achieve your new dream.

4. **PAST:** Refers to a past situation where you were rigid and inflexible. Can also hint at a time when you needed to embody the characteristics of the King.

5. **CROWN:** Intellect and logic are required to get to the heart of the matter. Indicates a father figure in your life.

6. **NEAR FUTURE:** A situation is at hand which you are capable of managing. You have the knowledge you need to assess the issue and make well-informed decisions. It can also suggest advice and unexpected help from someone with the King's attributes.

7. **FEAR:** A fear of authority or being locked into something. Fear of leaving freedom and frivolity behind to accept responsibilities.

8. **JUDGEMENT:** A powerful and feared individual that others respect.

9. **HOPE:** You dream of being in power and having responsibility and authority.

10. **OUTCOME:** You are well prepared for the next phase. Remain objective, and don't lower your standards for an easy win. You have what it takes to resolve conflicts and emerge successful. You might need to embrace the characteristics of the King to deal with the situation.

As a person, the King of Swords is self-disciplined, intelligent, and honest. He is rational, logical and a deep thinker. He does well in structured environments and can be stern. He may be an Air sign (Aquarius, Gemini or Libra).

OPPOSING CARDS

 **SEVEN OF CUPS**
self-indulgence
procrastination

REINFORCING CARDS

 **THREE OF WANDS**
forward planning,
ambition

COURT CARD PAIRS

KING OF SWORDS (intellectual) **KING OF PENTACLES** (unethical)

King of Swords
- helps the King of Pentacles by explaining the issue
- annoys the King of Pentacles when he is too theoretical

The Suit of Wands

The Suit of Wands is associated with energy, inspiration, determination, creativity, ambition and expansion.

If there are many Wands in a reading, the issue at hand is probably related to creativity and development. You may also be seeking meaning in your life.

The negative aspects of Wands include illusion, egotistical behaviour, a lack of direction or purpose, or impulsiveness.

Element: Fire

Keywords: impatient, adventurous, passionate, determined, creative

Corresponding playing card suit: Clubs

Astrological signs: Aries, Leo or Sagittarius

Noted for: passion and creativity

Ace of Wands

new ideas, creativity

Two of Wands

taking risks, discovery

Three of Wands

expansion, travel

Four of Wands

celebration, harmony

Five of Wands

disorganised, arguments

Six of Wands

acclaim, victory

Seven of Wands

challenge, competition

Eight of Wands
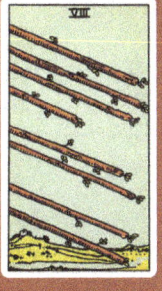
movement, progress

Nine of Wands

resilience, persistence

Ten of Wands

struggle, overload

Page of Wands

inspiration, discovery

Knight of Wands

energetic, passionate

Queen of Wands

capable, courageous

King of Wands

dramatic, bold

• CREATIVE ENERGY • INSPIRATION • ORIGINALITY • VISION • OPTIONS • CONCEPTION

Ace of Wands

DESCRIPTION
A hand in the clouds holds a wand. New leaves sprout from the wand, suggesting the potential for growth and inspiration. The green landscape in the background hints at creativity and the abundance of ideas. The castle represents upcoming opportunities. Mountains on the horizon suggest difficulties will be easily overcome.

The Ace of Wands symbolises a new beginning. Expect a surge of creative energy and new ideas. This card brings positivity, optimism and a spark of passion.

OVERVIEW
The Ace of Wands represents a creative idea that will lead to a new beginning. The birth of a concept or the beginning of a venture. This Ace is not passive, however, and requires that you take action to put things in motion. You should be feeling excited and filled with enthusiasm when this card appears.

LOVE
If you are in a relationship, this Ace suggests a new chapter brimming with excitement and new energy. It is a card of fertility, pregnancy and birth. If you are single, the Ace of Wands promises new beginnings.

CAREER
In a career spread, the Ace of Wands indicates the start of a new venture, brilliant ideas and an increase of creative energy. If you are looking for a job, it can indicate welcome news.

SPIRITUALITY
New beginnings on your spiritual path are suggested. Be open to new information and experiences.

ADVICE
Are you too consumed with your idea to listen to advice? Are you trying to bully others into helping? Reach for the stars, but be realistic about your limitations.

• BIRTH • ADVENTURE • BEGINNINGS • ACTIVITY • PASSION • ANTICIPATION

Celtic Cross Positions

1. **SIGNIFICATOR:** You are consumed by a new idea, project or concept. You have the ability to take this idea to the next level. You are entering a new phase.

2. **OBSTACLES:** If you have been reluctant to start a new project, this card advises you to stop procrastinating. The time to act is now. Taking the project further will lead to opportunities and growth.

3. **ROOT:** Represents the possibility of creativity, excitement and adventure. An idea has taken hold, urging you to act boldly.

4. **PAST:** Refers to a time when you took a chance on an idea, which likely is still affecting your life.

5. **CROWN:** Seize the initiative and let your enthusism carry you. A time of passion and creation.

6. **NEAR FUTURE:** Suggests a chance to be original and trust your own creative potential. Can also suggest pregnancy or the birth of a child. If there are issues, this card indicates that you'll discover creative ways of dealing with them.

7. **FEAR:** You fear lost opportunities and that your ideas will prove unsuccessful.

8. **JUDGEMENT:** A brave person who risks all to follow their dreams.

9. **HOPE:** Represents a hope for a more creative life.

10. **OUTCOME:** The seed of a new, exciting idea is sprouting. You are filled with inspiration and creativity. If you work hard, there is little doubt that you will be successful. Alternatively, someone might approach you with a creative idea. Be open to everything. Now is the time to initiate a new venture and to take chances.

OPPOSING CARDS

THE HANGED MAN
surrender, sacrifice, pause

FOUR OF CUPS
unmotivated, withdrawal

REINFORCING CARDS

WHEEL OF FORTUNE
a change in fortune

DEATH
change is coming

ACE-ACE PAIR

An Ace-Ace pair shows that a new spirit is entering your life. It draws on the energy of the Ace of Wands (creativity, excitement, adventure, courage), plus one of these:

ACE OF CUPS
deep feelings, intimacy, compassion, love

ACE OF PENTACLES
prosperity, abundance, trust, grounded

ACE OF SWORDS
intelligence, reason, justice, truth, clarity

1 Beginning

• PLANNING • TAKING RISKS • DECISIONS • RESTLESSNESS • WAITING • DIRECTION

Two of Wands

The Two of Wands represents an important decision. You are holding the world in your hands, and your future is full of opportunities, but you are cautious about taking the first step. Can also suggest a career change, promotion or international travel.

OVERVIEW
When the Two of Wands appears, you have a decision to make. You can either stay where you are or take a risk. Stepping out into the unknown will open up new potential. This card can represent emigration and business partnerships. It can also indicate a lack of contentment with your life.

LOVE
In a relationship, the Two of Wands hints that you might be feeling restless or considering becoming involved with a new partner. If you are single, this card suggests that you might need to decide between two potential lovers.

CAREER
In a career spread, this card indicates that it might be time to move from the planning to the implementation phase. The groundwork has been done; now is the time to put things in motion. It can also indicate a choice between two career options or possible travel for work.

SPIRITUALITY
The Two of Wands reminds us of the importance of spiritual balance.

ADVICE
Making a decision that will have such a big impact on your life isn't easy. But this card suggests now is the perfect time to take action. Be bold and courageous – you've got this!

DESCRIPTION
A man holds a globe and looks out over the ocean. He has the world is in his hands which suggests huge potential. He holds one staff in his hand. The other is attached to the wall, representing his reluctance to move from the planning phase to implementation. He stands within the castle walls, showing that he is not ready to make a move. Fruit on the wall represents abundance and the fertile land beyond also speaks of success. He only has to choose, and he will easily overcome any challenges that lie ahead.

• TWO PATHS • FIRST STEPS • EMIGRATION • ANTICIPATION • DISCOVERY • COURAGE

Celtic Cross Positions

1. **SIGNIFICATOR:** You are a creative person with huge potential. You might be feeling discontent or bored with your current life.

2. **OBSTACLES:** Procrastination stops you from moving forward. Make a plan of action.

3. **ROOT:** You are weighing up two ideas and unable to make a decision. This keeps you immobile.

4. **PAST:** Represents a past event where you took a chance. Perhaps you changed jobs, moved town or started a new venture.

5. **CROWN:** The bold, creative energy of this card suggests that you can achieve anything you set your mind to.

6. **NEAR FUTURE:** A choice lies before you, and it has the power to change your life. Only you will know what the right decision is. Don't make a choice simply because you are bored. Make sure this is what you really want.

7. **FEAR:** Represents fear of change or travel.

8. **JUDGEMENT:** People see you as a creative individual who has the power to take charge of their destiny.

9. **HOPE:** You hope you can find the courage to take the next step.

10. **OUTCOME:** A decision lies before you. You may already know your answer but feel scared to commit to your choice as you worry about making a mistake. Alternatively, if an opportunity is offered to you, grab it with both hands. Travel, education, creative energy…you are entering an exciting phase. You have the power to change your life.

OPPOSING CARDS

HIGH PRIESTESS
being passive, staying in the background

THE HIEROPHANT
conforming, going along with the group

EIGHT OF SWORDS
powerlessness, fear of action

TEN OF SWORDS
victim mentality, powerlessness

TEN OF PENTACLES
going by the rules, being conventional

REINFORCING CARDS

THE MAGICIAN
personal power, wielding a strong force

THE EMPEROR
authority

THE CHARIOT
personal power, command

THE SUN
vitality, brilliance, greatness

2 Duality, balance, harmony, reflection

• PROGRESS • EXPANSION • OPPORTUNITIES • ENTERPRISE • CONFIDENCE

Three of Wands

The Three of Wands represents being on the brink of a new adventure. It implies that you have planned carefully, worked hard, and can now watch everything come together. The realisation of goals, material success and accomplishment.

OVERVIEW
The Three of Wands represents hard work paying off. You are going in the right direction and are likely to be successful. It also hints at adventure and travel. If the previous card was about hesitation before taking a risk, this card is about expecting the rewards after the risk has been taken. An adventure lies ahead.

LOVE
This card suggests a healthy relationship, a long-distance relationship or moving abroad with your partner. If you are single, you are likely enjoying the freedom that this affords you.

CAREER
An auspicious card in any career spread, the Three of Wands represents ideas coming to fruition and dreams coming true. You are standing on the threshold of new horizons and possibilities. Your company may be considering expansion.

SPIRITUALITY
Spiritually, now is the time to follow your dream. Use your intuition and follow the path laid out before you.

ADVICE
Don't become so preoccupied with the future that you forget to live in the present.

DESCRIPTION
A man in red and green robes stands on a cliff. Three wands are planted in the ground around him, showing that his plans are stable and reliable. He looks out at the three ships sailing past. They represent the project he has just launched. The work is done; he now waits for his ships to return successfully. The water suggests movement and progress. From where he stands, he has a good view of what is happening around him, including any challenges or opportunities.

• INITIATIVE • FORESIGHT • TRAVEL • EXPLORATION • FORWARD PLANNING

Celtic Cross Positions

1. **SIGNIFICATOR:** You have the foresight, confidence and patience to see long-term projects through.

2. **OBSTACLES:** Things are now in motion and all you can do is watch. You might feel frustrated about not being able to take action.

3. **ROOT:** Recognise and evaluate your abilities. Your success may come in various forms and not necessarily in the way you expect.

4. **PAST:** Represents a past event where you were cautious and considered all options before taking action. This has paid off, and you are now reaping the benefits.

5. **CROWN:** You are filled with many creative concepts and ideas. You find it difficult to focus a single course of action.

6. **NEAR FUTURE:** Now is the time to turn your idea into reality. Planning and hard work will be required, but will also be rewarded. Travel might be on the horizon.

7. **FEAR:** You fear taking action without proper planning and analysis.

8. **JUDGEMENT:** Represents a successful individual with many business ventures or income streams. Often bursting with new ideas.

9. **HOPE:** Represents hope for travel or a successful business.

10. **OUTCOME:** Represents the potential for a successful outcome. With a bit more work, you could achieve your potential, not just financially but also spiritually. Things are coming together in a positive way.

OPPOSING CARDS

TWO OF SWORDS
avoiding the facts, staying stuck

TEN OF PENTACLES
being conservative, focusing on security

REINFORCING CARDS

THE FOOL
expanding horizons, unexplored territory

THE EMPEROR
leadership, providing direction

EIGHT OF CUPS
going on a trip, starting a journey

THREE OF PENTACLES
planning, preparing for the future

3 Trio, planning, ideas, creation

• CELEBRATION • JOY • HARMONY • RELAXATION • HOMECOMING • PROSPERITY • PEACE

Four of Wands

DESCRIPTION
A couple celebrate, holding up bouquets. In the foreground, four wands are firmly planted in the ground. A wreath of flowers and grapes is draped over them, representing success and harvest. An important goal has been achieved. Behind the couple, a crowd celebrates in front of a large castle, representing safety. The card has a happy, joyous feeling.

The Four of Wands represents a well-deserved rest after a busy time. It symbolises home and hearth, satisfaction in family and work life. It indicates that a level of success has been achieved. Can also imply that you are moving home.

OVERVIEW
The Four of Wands symbolises the happiness we feel after coming home after being away. Finally, surrounded by loved ones, we can relax and truly be ourselves. This card suggests that you deserve some time off to enjoy the simple things in life. If things have been difficult, this card indicates that better times lie ahead.

LOVE
A good card for those in relationships, as the Four of Wands represents a happy family. It also alludes to celebrations, so a party or ceremony may be on the horizon. It can also signify moving home. If you are single, the Four of Wands hints that you will soon find love.

CAREER
The Four of Wands suggests that things are going well in your career. Projects have been achieved, and milestones met. A productive and happy working environment. It can also signify graduation ceremonies, office gatherings or moving the office to a new location.

SPIRITUALITY
In a spiritual context, the Four of Wands suggests rituals, ceremonies, and other events within your community.

ADVICE
It is important to rest, relax, party and have fun. But don't lose sight of your goals. Keep an eye on your responsibilities as you enjoy time-out.

• FREEDOM • HOLIDAY • EMOTIONAL WARMTH • REUNION • HARVEST • SATISFACTION • SPONTANEITY

Celtic Cross Positions

1 SIGNIFICATOR: You have worked hard to get where you are, and feel proud of your achievements. Family and relationships are important to you.

2 OBSTACLES: You feel it is time to celebrate your achievements and take a break from routine.

3 ROOT: You are confident and feel emotionally and financially secure.

4 PAST: You have recently achieved something that you can be justly proud of. Perhaps a successful business venture or the successful completion of your studies.

5 CROWN: A time of rest and celebration. You feel proud of yourself and what you have achieved.

6 NEAR FUTURE: An upcoming celebration, such as a reunion, wedding or birth. Creative endeavours are successful.

7 FEAR: You fear commitment.

8 JUDGEMENT: Represents a prosperous person who is looked upon with envy. It seems they have everything they want – financial success and a happy partnership.

9 HOPE: Family lies at the heart of your desires.

10 OUTCOME: An event or celebration that will bring light, laughter and excitement into your life. Successful outcomes, possibly a holiday. It can also indicate that it is time to let go of things that no longer serve you – a relationship, job or even negative emotions.

OPPOSING CARDS

THE DEVIL
bondage, lack of freedom

TEN OF WANDS
burdens, being in an oppressive situation

FOUR OF CUPS
apathy, flat feeling, lack of excitement

SIX OF SWORDS
mild depression, little to celebrate

EIGHT OF SWORDS
restriction, lack of freedom

REINFORCING CARDS

THREE OF CUPS
excitement, high spirits, celebration

TWO OF PENTACLES
fun, parties, excitement

4 Stability, order, making things happen

• DISAGREEMENTS • COMPETITION • TENSION • DIVERSITY • RIVALRY • CONFLICT OF INTEREST

Five of Wands

The Five of Wands represents competition, disorder and struggle. The figures on the card are a disorganised group trying to build something. You need to take charge and get your act together. It also indicates power struggles, rivalry and conflict.

OVERVIEW
The Five of Wands represents a struggle of some kind and the disappointment that follows when things don't work out as planned. Competition and the clashing of egos can be expected. This card serves as a reminder of the value of patience in adversity. The situation is not necessarily dire; it is just a bump in the road that needs to be smoothed out.

LOVE
In a relationship, the Five of Wands hints at misunderstandings and arguments. If you are single, this card can suggest rivalry and competition in your pursuit of someone's affection.

CAREER
In the workplace, you might find yourself clashing with colleagues or being overly competitive. You might feel challenged and judged by others.

SPIRITUALITY
Conflict might be preventing your spiritual side from flourishing.

ADVICE
Competition can be positive because it encourages us to improve, but it can also leave us feeling deflated, frustrated and worthless. Try not to take things too seriously and remain playful and flexible.

DESCRIPTION
Five men are unsuccessfully trying to build something. They are not working well together, and seem to be working against each other. Each man wears a different outfit, showing their discord and different backgrounds. There is no communication between them. It seems as though their egos stop them from being constructive and working together.

• DIFFERENCES • DISORGANISED • CHALLENGES • CLASHING EGOS • MINOR SETBACKS

Celtic Cross Positions

1. **SIGNIFICATOR:** You stand up for what you believe in, even if it makes you unpopular. You can be a bit too confrontational.

2. **OBSTACLES:** The situation can be resolved if you take charge and express yourself clearly.

3. **ROOT:** You may feel as though everything and everyone is against you. Nothing seems to work in your favour.

4. **PAST:** Refers to a recent conflict or argument which is still relevant. Perhaps it has yet to be resolved.

5. **CROWN:** Imbalance and conflict of interest hinder progress. Many different egos are at play, and it is difficult to make sense of things.

6. **NEAR FUTURE:** You are entering a phase of rivalry and conflict. Travel plans might be affected. Frustrating times lie ahead.

7. **FEAR:** Represents a fear of being misunderstood or of losing a battle.

8. **JUDGEMENT:** A competitive individual who enjoys overcoming challenges and winning arguments.

9. **HOPE:** You hope things will come together in an organised and amiable way. You hope for the success of a project.

10. **OUTCOME:** Competition, rivalry and arguments are in your future. Other peoples' opinions might conflict with yours. Keep patient, be flexible and try not to lose your temper. This is likely to pass quickly.

OPPOSING CARDS

TEMPERANCE
balance, agreement, working together

THE WORLD
integration, working together

TWO OF CUPS
truce, agreement, coming together

TWO OF PENTACLES
working smoothly, getting people together

THREE OF PENTACLES
teamwork, cooperation

REINFORCING CARDS

SEVEN OF WANDS
opposition, fighting

TEN OF WANDS
struggle, hassles, meeting resistance

FIVE OF SWORDS
discord, people set against each other

5 Adaptation, challenge, conflict

• SUCCESS • ACCLAIM • TRIUMPH • PUBLIC RECOGNITION • PROGRESS • SELF-CONFIDENCE • VICTORY

Six of Wands

The Six of Wands represents reward, good news and achievement. You have reached a significant goal and can bask in the glory for a moment. You may receive recognition, reward and acclaim for your recent success.

OVERVIEW
You are being honoured for a recent achievement. You have triumphed and achieved a level of success. You may have received an award, a promotion or feel that you have achieved. A big confidence boost. This moment is temporary as there is more work to be done, but you deserve this moment of recognition.

LOVE
If you are in a relationship, the Six of Wands suggests a partnership that works well together. If you are single, there is a chance that you'll meet an ideal partner soon.

CAREER
Success and victory are promised when you see this card In a career spread. You've worked hard and have achieved what you set out to do. A promotion, pay raise or an exciting new opportunity are all possibilities. People look at you with admiration. You are seen as a natural leader.

SPIRITUALITY
In a spiritual context, people are likely looking to you for leadership or advice.

ADVICE
It's easy to feel superior when you've had success. This card reminds you that your moment on the top will be temporary. Be proud of yourself but don't become conceited.

DESCRIPTION
A man rides on a white horse through a crowd. He wears a victory laurel, and carries another on his wand. These represent his success and achievement. The horse is a symbol of nobility, speed and freedom and is generally associated with conquering power. The crowd cheers for him as he travels past victoriously.

• GOOD NEWS • PROMOTION • FAME • ACHIEVEMENT • REWARD • BREAKTHROUGH

Celtic Cross Positions

1 **SIGNIFICATOR:** You are successful but need to remain humble.

2 **OBSTACLES:** You will successfully navigate the situation at hand if you stay focused and trust yourself.

3 **ROOT:** Your ego prevents you from seeing the situation clearly. Nothing will be resolved until you treat others with respect and realise their value.

4 **PAST:** Represents a huge success that changed your life. You learnt important lessons that are still valuable to you. Don't wish for the past, but look to the future instead.

5 **CROWN:** Good news, possibly a promotion or financial success.

6 **NEAR FUTURE:** Expect success, but know that more work is required for long-term security. You might receive acclaim.

7 **FEAR:** Represents a fear of public speaking. Also a fear that things might not go as planned.

8 **JUDGEMENT:** Represents a successful person who has worked hard to get where they are.

9 **HOPE:** You desire to be recognised for your achievements.

10 **OUTCOME:** Your success will lead to reward and acknowledgement for a job well done. Celebrate and enjoy the moment, but do not become complacent or conceited.

OPPOSING CARDS

THE TOWER
humility,
loss of acclaim

FIVE OF CUPS
loss,
defeat

TEN OF SWORDS
self-deprecating,
feeling down

FOUR OF PENTACLES
alone,
loves money

FIVE OF PENTACLES
rejection,
lack of recognition

REINFORCING CARDS

THE CHARIOT
triumph,
self-confidence

THE SUN
acclaim,
prominence

NINE OF CUPS
self-satisfaction,
achieving what you want

6 Patterns, togetherness

• CHALLENGE • COMPETITION • PROTECTION • PERSEVERANCE • SPIRIT • VALOUR • DEFIANCE

Seven of Wands

DESCRIPTION
A man atop a hill holds a wand, fighting off six more wands. He stands alone on top and is, therefore, in a position of advantage. He seems to be defending his position successfully. His two shoes are different, suggesting he might not have had time to prepare for this battle.

The Seven of Wands suggests taking a stand for your beliefs. It can also represent an internal or external struggle. It carries the feeling that you are being tested.

OVERVIEW
In a general context, the Seven of Wands indicates confrontation and the chance to defend your beliefs. It represents believing in yourself, knowing your purpose, and not being afraid to fight for what you believe is right. It can also indicate that you are struggling against something internal that you must come to terms with before moving on.

LOVE
Not a good card for those in a relationship, as it suggests challenges, conflicting interests and arguments. If you are single, the Seven of Wands indicates that you might have to fight for the person you want.

CAREER
In a career spread, this card represents obstacles and difficulties. You may have to defend your morals or judgment. A battle, competition, and rivalry are all possible. Don't take on any unnecessary fights. Understand your conviction and motives before taking a firm stand.

SPIRITUALITY
This card implies that you might need to defend your spiritual beliefs.

ADVICE
Make sure of your motives before you enter the arena. Don't get sucked into unnecessary arguments. Not everyone has to agree with your decisions.

• STRUGGLING • FIGHTING • COURAGE • TEST • OPPOSITION • TAKING A STAND

Celtic Cross Positions

1 **SIGNIFICATOR:** You believe in yourself and your ability to handle the situation.

2 **OBSTACLES:** You want to stand up for your beliefs but feel insecure and unable to decide.

3 **ROOT:** Represents facing the choice of whether to stand your ground or not. You have to decide what's important and choose your battle. Not all of them are worth fighting.

4 **PAST:** A recent time when you had to stand up for something you believed in. This wasn't easy, but you are proud of yourself for standing firm. It likely led to a positive outcome.

5 **CROWN:** You will soon need to defend your motivations and decisions. Those who are against you are gathering. Prepare yourself.

6 **NEAR FUTURE:** You have worked hard and will soon need to fight for what you believe in. Choose where to invest your time and energy. Be honest with yourself about what you want, and don't let petty arguments distract you.

7 **FEAR:** You fear defeat or confrontation.

8 **JUDGEMENT:** Represents a successful person who might be envied by others.

9 **HOPE:** You desire to win this fight.

10 **OUTCOME:** You have no choice but to face the coming conflict. Others might be jealous of your success and will put obstacles in your path. Hold true to yourself and have the confidence to stand your ground. You are likely to succeed.

OPPOSING CARDS

HIGH PRIESTESS
being passive, holding back

THE HANGED MAN
waiting, letting go

THREE OF PENTACLES
teamwork

REINFORCING CARDS

FIVE OF WANDS
opposition, fighting

NINE OF WANDS
defending your position, refusing to yield

FIVE OF SWORDS
me-against-them mentality, conflict

7 Accomplishments, self-expansion

• MOVEMENT • FAST PACE • CHANGE • TRAVEL • ACTION • SUCCESS • RUSHING AHEAD

Eight of Wands

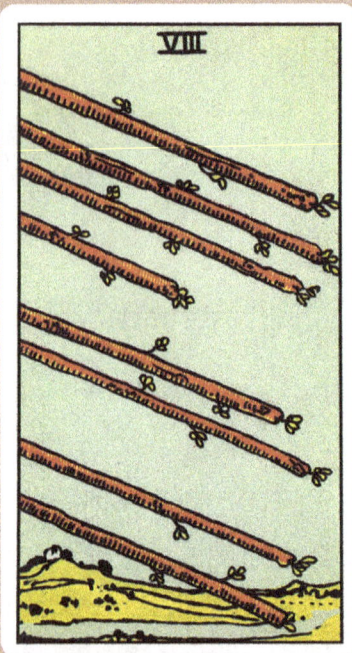

The Eight of Wands brings movement and energy into your life. It speaks of events unfolding rapidly and sudden plans and ideas. Travel, especially unexpected, is also possible.

DESCRIPTION
Eight wands fly through the air. All of them have sprouting leaves that suggest new growth and ideas. The sky is clear, representing no immediate challenges. The landscape is fertile, hinting at being filled with creative ideas and promise. The flowing river offers insight and life.

OVERVIEW
The Eight of Wands brings excitement into your life. Things are moving quickly when it appears and it is time for hasty action. Excitement, new projects and ventures, quick developments and promises may all be on offer. You might receive some unexpected news or be swept off your feet.

LOVE
Whether single or in a relationship, exciting times are ahead for you. This card suggests movement, progress and infatuation.

CAREER
In a career spread, things are moving quickly towards reaching your goal. You are being swept along with the motion and can expect success. There is a sense of urgency and speed. A new venture, an exciting idea, sudden action. Travelling for work is also indicated. However, this card suggests you should not make decisions without careful thought.

SPIRITUALITY
Your spiritual life is likely flooded with positive energy.

ADVICE
The speed at which things are happening might make you feel pressured to make a quick decision. But make time for careful consideration, and only decide when you feel ready.

• END OF PHASE • PROGRESS • ACTIVITY • HASTINESS • SPEED • OPTIONS • EXCITING TIMES

Celtic Cross Positions

1. **SIGNIFICATOR:** You are brimming with ideas, but are cautioned not to make decisions without careful deliberation.

2. **OBSTACLES:** Choices, new information and ideas make you feel overwhelmed. Take the time you need to make an informed decision.

3. **ROOT:** Events are now in motion, and there is no turning back. The only way is forward.

4. **PAST:** Represents a time when you acted rashly and regret this. It can also refer to a recent time of great excitement that is affecting the present situation.

5. **CROWN:** If life is feeling stagnant, this card indicates that movement is coming, possibly from an unexpected direction. New energy, ideas and opportunities are on the way.

6. **NEAR FUTURE:** New information will change your course. Be mindful that things may not be what they seem. Look for the truth and try not to be distracted by everything on offer.

7. **FEAR:** You have a fear of being too hasty in making decisions.

8. **JUDGEMENT:** Represents an impulsive and busy individual.

9. **HOPE:** Represents a desire for success or creating something positive.

10. **OUTCOME:** Movement and excitement will enter your life. Ideas and creative energy surge through you. Possible travel. A decision will need to be made. You have the energy to see a new project through to completion.

OPPOSING CARDS

HIGH PRIESTESS
waiting, holding off

FOUR OF SWORDS
not rushing in, preparing

SEVEN OF PENTACLES
assessment, taking stock before acting

REINFORCING CARDS

THE FOOL
taking risks

THE MAGICIAN
taking action, making things happen

WHEEL OF FORTUNE
rapid pace, quick developments

DEATH
conclusion, endings

EIGHT OF CUPS
finishing up, ending a chapter

KNIGHT OF SWORDS
movement, activity

8 Inspiration, structure, balance

• RESILIENCE • COURAGE • PERSISTENCE • TEST OF FAITH • BOUNDARIES • STRENGTH

Nine of Wands

The Nine of Wands represents a recent struggle that has left you bruised. Despite feeling exhausted, you stand ready to defend yourself again if necessary. The defence you have built gives you the security to take a moment to consolidate. Not the time for making progress.

DESCRIPTION
An injured man stands in a circle of wands. You get the feeling that he's just been in a battle. He clutches a wand as he looks over his shoulder. He seems to be preparing for the next onslaught. He is tired but well-prepared for this final challenge. Because of his defences, the next assault will not be a surprise – he will see the enemy coming.

OVERVIEW
When the Nine of Wands appears, you are likely feeling drained from a recent battle. You are close to achieving what you want, but the struggle has left you demoralised. This card advises you to take some time out before pushing forward. When you are ready to move, you are likely to be successful. It also implies that you might be suffering from a lack of confidence or that you do not have faith in yourself.

LOVE
Not an ideal card for those in a relationship as it implies a difficult time. If you are considering ending the relationship, this card encourages you to keep going. If you are single, you might still be wounded from a recent failed relationship.

CAREER
Although this card represents difficulty, it is an auspicious career card. Yes, you are halfway through a battle, and there are more troubles to come. But most of the hard work is done, and you are close to success. Take this moment to breathe, make sure your territory is well-defended, and prepare for the final challenge.

SPIRITUALITY
In a spiritual context, the Nine of Wands indicates you have learnt the required lesson, and now is the time to move on.

ADVICE
Don't be too wary and cautious that you forget to see the good in people. Make sure you are not being too defensive.

• ENDURANCE • LAST STAND • STAMINA • BATTLE WEARY • FATIGUE • FIGHT YOUR CORNER

Celtic Cross Positions

1. **SIGNIFICATOR:** You may feel trapped, but the feelings are possibly of your own making. Find out what is making you feel this way.

2. **OBSTACLES:** Do not defend an idea or position that no longer needs defending. Analyse the situation. If there's a task you have been avoiding, now is the time to handle it.

3. **ROOT:** A warning to proceed carefully. Keep looking over your shoulder and expect the worst.

4. **PAST:** Represents a time when much effort was required. It wasn't easy, but you emerged successful, even if a bit bruised.

5. **CROWN:** Everyone and everything seems to be against you. But you have the strength and reserves to stand your ground. Suspicion and caution is needed.

6. **NEAR FUTURE:** Represents gathering of strength before a battle. Take the time you need to get ready. If you are well-prepared, you are likely to be successful.

7. **FEAR:** You fear being caught unprepared.

8. **JUDGEMENT:** Represents someone who decides to stand their ground, whatever the cost.

9. **HOPE:** You hope for success and peace.

10. **OUTCOME:** Expect another battle before this situation is over. Stand your ground and fight for what you believe in. This card tells you that you will succeed.

OPPOSING CARDS

THREE OF CUPS
friendship, trusting someone

SIX OF CUPS
innocence, believing the best

EIGHT OF CUPS
weariness, fatigue

REINFORCING CARDS

STRENGTH
endurance, resolve, heart

SEVEN OF WANDS
defending a position, holding out

TWO OF SWORDS
being defensive, closing yourself off

SEVEN OF PENTACLES
pause in work to consolidate

EIGHT OF PENTACLES
persistence

9 Concepts come together

• STRUGGLE • STRAIN • OVERLOADED • UPROOTING • HEAVY BURDEN • GOAL IN SIGHT

Ten of Wands

DESCRIPTION
A man carries ten wands in front of him and, therefore, cannot see where he is going. His back is bent, implying that the load is heavy and that he is tired. The buildings in the distance show that he is nearly at his destination and will soon be able to release his burden.

10 Completion, success, transformation

The Ten of Wands indicates that you are overburdened with demands and are carrying a lot of responsibility. However, this will be short-lived. You're nearly at the finish line.

OVERVIEW
You are carrying a heavy load and need to find ways to lighten it. You have taken on too much, either because you don't trust anyone else, are too willing to please, or unable to say no. It can also refer to a situation that started out manageable but has now grown. The card suggests that you need to delegate and perhaps lower your expectations. You are nearing the end, so make sure you have enough reserves and resources to see this through.

LOVE
If you are in a relationship, this card suggests you feel overburdened. Perhaps your partner relies on you too heavily. It might also imply that your relation is suffering from stress. If you are single, this card suggests you are too drained and exhausted for a new relationship.

CAREER
In a career sense, this card hints that you've taken on more than you can manage. You are struggling with increased work hours, a change in responsibilities, or a project that has grown. You are in danger of burnout and must find a way to spread the load. You may also need to find a creative solution to the problem.

SPIRITUALITY
The Ten of Wands, in a spiritual sense, suggests that you've been too bogged down with mundane matters and that you've lost your enthusiasm.

ADVICE
You might be adding stress and pressure by taking on more than you can handle, having unrealistic expectations, or being unable to say no. If you've taken on responsibilities that you can no longer handle, you need to let them go.

• RESPONSIBILITIES • PROBLEMS • WEIGHT ON SHOULDERS • DRUDGERY • DEMANDS

Celtic Cross Positions

1 SIGNIFICATOR: You feel the weight of responsibility and find it difficult to keep your eyes on the goal.

2 OBSTACLES: You are carrying too many responsibilities and need to lighten your load. Learn to delegate and stop being a perfectionist.

3 ROOT: You are pushing yourself too hard. Make time to have fun.

4 PAST: Represents feeling trapped and weighed down. A previous overwhelming burden is still affecting you.

5 CROWN: You feel stuck in your situation and cannot see a way out.

6 NEAR FUTURE: You are going through a period where you feel overloaded with responsibilities, demands and burdens. Delegate and release what you can.

7 FEAR: You fear working too hard for little gain. You fear that a project will fail.

8 JUDGEMENT: Represents a hard worker who takes on more than they can handle.

9 HOPE: You are tired and carrying a heavy burden. You wish to complete the job and rest for a while.

10 OUTCOME: You need to take responsibility to see the job through. You are nearly at the finish line and need to knuckle down and prepare for the final push. Break the task into manageable steps and get help where you can. Keep your focus and continue to move forward. Success is nearly yours.

OPPOSING CARDS

THE FOOL
carefree, living in the moment

THE HANGED MAN
letting go

FOUR OF WANDS
free of burdens, escaping oppression

FOUR OF SWORDS
relaxing, resting

SEVEN OF SWORDS
avoiding responsibility

REINFORCING CARDS

JUSTICE
accountability, responsibility

FIVE OF WANDS
struggle, hassles, resistance

SIX OF SWORDS
getting by, struggling along

NINE OF SWORDS
worrying

FIVE OF PENTACLES
struggling, hard times

• INSPIRATION • DISCOVERY • POTENTIAL • FREE SPIRIT • ENTHUSIASM • EXCITEMENT

Page of Wands

The Page of Wands indicates that life is about to get exciting. Fresh energy is blowing into your life, bringing ideas, potential, creativity and a general spark. You'll be feeling rejuvenated and enthusiastic when this card appears. Indicates good news.

OVERVIEW
The Page of Wands suggests that life is about to take an exciting turn. Perhaps you'll get a brilliant idea that sends your career in a new direction, meet someone who ignites childlike passion in you, have an opportunity to travel or receive surprising news. A time of playfulness.

LOVE
For those in a relationship, this card suggests that you and your partner are happy and have found ways to keep your relationship exciting. If you are single, now is a great time to get out and meet new people.

CAREER
In a career context, the Page of Wands indicates a new, exciting project or job. A spark has been lit and is carrying you forward. You are excited to get up in the mornings and move things along. Can also represent travel and good news in the form of salary increases and promotions.

SPIRITUALITY
In a spiritual reading, this card indicates going in a new direction or meeting new people with similar interests.

ADVICE
Dropping everything for the sake of a fascinating new person or venture might seem exciting, but you could end up with half-finished projects. Find the commitment to see things through.

DESCRIPTION
A young man holds a wand in both hands. His tunic is decorated with salamanders, symbolising fire and transformation. He stands still, suggesting that although inspired, he has not yet taken action. Green leaves sprout from the wand, implying creativity and growth. The desert landscape suggests he is able to find growth in the most unlikely places and is not limited by his circumstances.

• INVENTIVE • MESSAGES • FRESH IDEAS • TRAVEL • EXCITING NEWS • NEW PHASE

Celtic Cross Positions

1. **SIGNIFICATOR:** You are full of creative energy and are ready to start new ventures.

2. **OBSTACLES:** You are bursting with ideas. Life feels exciting. Enthusiasm carries you forward.

3. **ROOT:** Doors have recently been opened for you. A new idea has led you to this opportunity, or an unexpected message has taken you by surprise.

4. **PAST:** Represents a person who deeply affected your life. Male or female, this person's childlike energy and optimism inspired you.

5. **CROWN:** Your inability to finish projects has led to this situation.

6. **NEAR FUTURE:** Exciting news or fresh ideas are heading your way. This card promises the beginning of a new phase. Life is about to become busy. Grab the opportunities being offered.

7. **FEAR:** You fear stagnation or running out of steam.

8. **JUDGEMENT:** Represents an energetic person, full of creative ideas.

9. **HOPE:** You hope for exciting changes, successful projects or good news.

10. **OUTCOME:** An exciting change is coming your way. This could include travel, moving house, a new relationship, an exciting new venture or a promotion. This card suggests that you are ready for the change, but reminds you of the importance of committing to long-term goals.

As a person, the Page of Wands is active, optimistic and full of energy. Someone who is trustworthy, loyal and brimming with ideas. They tend to rush into things without thinking and to get bored easily. They may be a fire sign (Aries, Leo or Sagittarius).

OPPOSING CARDS

 **TEMPERANCE** balance, moderation

 **THE TOWER** catastrophe, destruction

REINFORCING CARDS

 **WHEEL OF FORTUNE** rapid change, movement

 **THE WORLD** fulfilment, success

 **EIGHT OF WANDS** travel, movement

• ENERGY • PASSION • ACTION • ADVENTURE • MOVEMENT • IMPULSIVE

Knight of Wands

The Knight of Wands brings movement and adventure to your life. A great deal of excitement can be expected — a new friend or lover, a house move or a new hobby.

DESCRIPTION

The Knight sits on his horse. He wears full armour decorated with salamanders (symbols of fire, faith and indestructibility). The wand he holds sprouts leaves, representing the energy and creativity he feels. His horse is poised and ready for action. The hot desert landscape does not dampen his spirits.

OVERVIEW
In a general context, the Knight of Wands suggests that things are going better than expected. Ventures are successful, and you are full of confidence. Now is a good time to put new ideas into motion. This card also indicates the power that lies in finishing what you started. The Knight can be rebellious, so check your motives.

LOVE
If you are in a relationship, your partner might share traits with the Knight of Wands. Your relationship is probably exciting and full of energy. If you are single, perhaps you'll meet someone who reminds you of the Knight's passionate nature.

CAREER
In a career reading, things are likely to be moving – you might be changing jobs, launching a new business or starting a new project. This card brings the intense excitement that comes with new creative energy. Can also indicate travelling for work.

SPIRITUALITY
The Knight of Wands indicates that you have begun a new spiritual practice that energises you.

ADVICE
You're the life and soul of the party, but if people can't rely on you, you will start to lose your charm.

• DARING • IMPATIENT • TRAVEL • CHANGE • EXCITEMENT • MOVING HOME

Celtic Cross Positions

1. **SIGNIFICATOR:** Your longing for change causes you to rush headlong into things without considering the consequences.

2. **OBSTACLES:** If you are debating your path and doubting yourself, this card advises you to push through.

3. **ROOT:** Lots of energy creates endless possibilities that distract you. You might need to step back and put things into perspective before deciding where to spend your time and energy.

4. **PAST:** Represents a time when you pursued your goal relentlessly. Perhaps you were foolhardy, rebellious and vain. Things might not have ended as you wished.

5. **CROWN:** Your life is brimming with excitement. A warning not to be too impulsive.

6. **NEAR FUTURE:** If you are currently feeling bored, this will soon change. You are about to be swept forward with the motion of the Knight. Travel, new projects and meeting people are all indicated.

7. **FEAR:** Represents fear of travel and change. You may lack confidence.

8. **JUDGEMENT:** Represents someone who embodies the Knight's characteristics and is always up for a new challenge, idea or adventure.

9. **HOPE:** You desire change, movement and excitement. You might be hoping for a clever idea that will solve a problem.

10. **OUTCOME:** Things are likely moving fast. Significant change and excitement are coming. Now is the time to put ideas into action, take risks and try something different. You might have visitors from abroad or go travelling. Whatever challenges arise, the Knight suggests that you can easily handle them.

As a person, the Knight of Wands is charming, adventurous and exciting. He is impulsive and blunt, but his energy and enthusiasm endear people to him. His temper is legendary. He may be a fire sign (Aries, Leo or Sagittarius).

OPPOSING CARDS

 **FOUR OF SWORDS** retreat, contemplation

REINFORCING CARDS

 **THE MAGICIAN** action, movement

COURT CARD PAIRS

KNIGHT OF WANDS (restless)   **QUEEN OF PENTACLES** (constant)

Knight of Wands
- teaches the Queen how to enjoy herself
- annoys the Queen by constantly being busy

• CAPABLE • VERSATILE • FAITHFUL • DYNAMIC • ATTRACTIVE • MAGNETIC • ENERGETIC

Queen of Wands

The Queen of Wands is a dynamic, confident woman. When she appears, it is time to take charge of your life. She seems to balance work and home life effortlessly, and might be encouraging you to do the same. Charity work, a new career or a hobby — decide where you want to go and start heading in that direction.

OVERVIEW
In a general context, the Queen of Wands suggests that you'll be accomplishing many tasks seamlessly. This card represents taking charge and getting organised. The Queen isn't a victim or martyr, she gets things done. She fiercely defends her friends and family if she feels they have been wronged. You might need to stand up for someone in trouble. If you feel called to get involved with a charity or volunteer work, now is a good time to sign up.

LOVE
If you are in a relationship, the Queen of Wands can indicate that your partner embodies the Queen's qualities. If you are single, you might meet someone who reminds you of the Queen.

CAREER
In a career reading, this card indicates a time of great achievement and energy. Things are getting done, clients and customers are happy, and profits are healthy. It can also mean you will receive guidance from someone with the Queen's qualities.

SPIRITUALITY
You may be on a quest to expand your spiritual knowledge.

ADVICE
Your strength and capability come naturally to you, but you might be smothering the development of those around you. Look around and make sure that everyone has the opportunity to shine.

DESCRIPTION
The Queen sits on a throne, wearing a yellow gown (associated with brightness and enlightenment). The throne is decorated with lions (symbolising courage and strength). Sunflowers, representing life, fertility, joy and satisfaction, are depicted on her throne, crown, and in her left hand. She holds a wand with sprouting leaves in her right hand, representing new ideas and growth. A black cat sits at her feet, showing the Queen's affinity with all things feminine.

• QUICK TEMPERED • COURAGEOUS • PASSIONATE • STRONG-WILLED • INDEPENDENT • CONFIDENT

Celtic Cross Positions

1 SIGNIFICATOR: You are inspired by new creative ideas and plans. Tantalised by the possibilities that have opened up.

2 OBSTACLES: You are in a process of self-discovery and will find your leadership qualities.

3 ROOT: You likely enjoy your career and are good at communicating. The Queen's characteristics might be useful in negotiating the current situation.

4 PAST: Represents someone who embodies the Queen's qualities and was helpful in a desperate situation. Could also refer to a time you fiercely defended someone you loved.

5 CROWN: You give your time to others freely, but now might be a good time to do something for yourself. A bit of self-care will make everything seem more manageable.

6 NEAR FUTURE: You may be called to get involved in a cause or charity that leads to positive change, new developments and exciting possibilities.

7 FEAR: Represents a fear of losing your good looks or your temper.

8 JUDGEMENT: Represents a confident person, full of creative flair and charisma.

9 HOPE: You desire a family and a successful career.

10 OUTCOME: You will soon be in a situation where it is crucial that you make a powerful impression – perhaps in a job interview or a presentation. The Queen suggests that you'll manage this seamlessly. Make sure your current path and future vision are aligned. If changes are necessary, let your intuition guide you.

As a person, the Queen of Wands is energetic, vivacious, passionate and has a magnetic personality. She goes after what she wants. She does not suffer fools and has a temper. She may be a fire sign (Aries, Leo or Sagittarius).

OPPOSING CARDS

 **STRENGTH** patience, calm, discipline

 **TEMPERANCE** self-restraint, calm

COURT CARD PAIRS

QUEEN OF WANDS (cheerful)   **KNIGHT OF SWORDS** (serious)

Queen of Wands
- teaches the Knight to be passionate and outgoing
- annoys the Knight when incompetence doesn't bother her

• POWERFUL • DRAMATIC • IDEAS • NOBLE • ENDURANCE • ENTHUSIASM • PASSION

King of Wands

The King of Wands is passionate and powerful. He suggests you have the ability, intellect and leadership potential to take charge of the situation. His lively energy prevents the atmosphere from becoming too serious and oppressive.

OVERVIEW
In a general context, the King of Wands suggests that you have the energy, experience and enthusiasm to achieve your current goal. You have the ability to motivate others and lead the way. Friends may come to you for advice or look up to you. Your ambition is strong enough to carry you to a successful outcome.

LOVE
In a relationship, your partner may have the King of Wand's qualities. The King can be a passionate lover but values his freedom. If you are single, you may meet someone who reminds you of the King.

CAREER
This card suggests that things are going well in your career. You are successful, ambitious and motivated. Everything is slotting into place. You may be in a leadership position or might be asked to step into a situation where you have more control over others. You need to express your wishes and ideas clearly.

SPIRITUALITY
The King of Wands reminds you of the importance of trusting your intuition and believing in yourself.

ADVICE
You often find yourself involved in power plays or using power negatively. You'll need to deal with these issues before you can achieve your goal. Others model themselves against you, so you are under pressure to set a good example.

DESCRIPTION
The King sits on his throne. In his right hand, he holds a wand sprouting new leaves, symbolising growth and creativity. His throne and cloak are decorated with lions and salamanders (symbols of fire, courage and strength). The salamanders biting their own tails represent infinity.

• CHARMING • FRIENDLY • QUICK DECISIONS • ENERGETIC • BOLD • OPTIMISTIC • CONFIDENT

Celtic Cross Positions

1 SIGNIFICATOR: You have significant influence over others. Take care not to manipulate or overwhelm them.

2 OBSTACLES: You have more power or knowledge than you credit yourself with. You have what you need to solve this issue.

3 ROOT: You have learnt a lot, grown and evolved. You have the ability to view the situation from different perspectives.

4 PAST: Represents a time when you took risks, believed in yourself and emerged successful. It can also suggest that you received help and support from someone with the King's qualities.

5 CROWN: You are a good leader. Others look to you to lead the way.

6 NEAR FUTURE: You will likely succeed at whatever you put your energy into. This card suggests that now is a good time to take a few carefully calculated risks.

7 FEAR: You fear failure.

8 JUDGEMENT: Represents a charismatic and confident individual. A born leader.

9 HOPE: You desire to be recognised or given a chance at leadership.

10 OUTCOME: Represents a positive outcome. Fortune favours the bold, so now is the time to go after what you want. A windfall or successful negotiations are indicated. Grab opportunities with both hands. Work passionately on your current project. Keep your eye on the goal and follow your dream.

As a person, the King of Wands is confident, motivated, energetic, optimistic and a natural leader. He is friendly, funny and charming. He can be self-centred and hot-tempered. He may be a fire sign (Aries, Leo or Sagittarius).

OPPOSING CARDS

 **FOUR OF PENTACLES** resistant to change, stagnation

REINFORCING CARDS

 **THE CHARIOT** endurance, ambition, triumph

COURT CARD PAIRS

KING OF WANDS (forceful)   **QUEEN OF CUPS** (gentle)

King of Wands
- teaches the Queen to be more assertive
- annoys the Queen because he assumes she will follow him

www.ingramcontent.com/pod-product-compliance
Lightning Source LLC
Chambersburg PA
CBHW081131170426
43197CB00017B/2826